# The Antiracist Kitchen

## 21 STORIES (AND RECIPES)

# The Antiracist Kitchen

## 21 STORIES (AND RECIPES)

edited by
**Nadia L. Hohn**

illustrated by
**Roza Nozari**

ORCA BOOK PUBLISHERS

# CONTENTS

**Foreword** by Ainara Alleyne    vii

**Introduction** by Nadia L. Hohn    1
*Recipe: Cornmeal Porridge*    5

## Chapter One
### Reclaim: *How We Take Back What Is Ours*    7

**Beans on the Stove, Corn Bread on the Table** by Andrea L. Rogers    11
*Recipe: Bean Soup (Tuya Ugama)*    14

**Love Me, Love My Banana Fritters** by Hasani Claxton    17
*Recipe: Banana Fritters*    19

**Tortillas con Queso (and Love)** by Jennifer De Leon    21
*Recipe: Tortillas con Queso*    25

**Fusion Fried Plantain** by Janice Lynn Mather    27
*Recipe: Fusion Fried Plantain*    30

**Manoomin** by Waubgeshig Rice    33
*Recipe: Wild Rice with Corn and Mushrooms*    37

## Chapter Two
### Resist: *How We Respond to Injustice*    39

**The True Story behind Ketchup Pizza** by S.K. Ali    43
*Recipe: Ketchup Pizza*    46

**Grandma's Greens Chase the Blues Away** by Bryan Patrick Avery    49
*Recipe: Bryan's Old-Fashioned Collard Greens*    52

**A Cake for My Bully** by Natasha Deen    55
*Recipe: A Cake*    57

**The Best Deviled Eggs Ever** by Andrea J. Loney    59
*Recipe: Southern-Style Deviled Eggs*    63

**Girl Scout Breakfast** by Linda Sue Park    65
*Recipe: Fried Bologna*    69

**Muhammara** by Danny Ramadan    71
*Recipe: Muhammara*    74

## Chapter Three

### Restore: *How We Create Healing Space for Ourselves and Others*

**What's for Lunch?** by Marty Chan — 81
*Recipe: My Mom's Chinese Dumplings (War Teep)* — 85

**On Belonging** by Reyna Grande — 87
*Recipe: Taquitos de Papa (Little Potato Tacos)* — 91

**Sharing Life's Sweetness** by Simran Jeet Singh — 93
*Recipe: Kheer* — 96

**In Defense of the Humble Rice** by Ann Yu-Kyung Choi — 99
*Recipe: Tasty and Easy Kimbap* — 103

**A Reimagined Malawach** by Ayelet Tsabari — 105
*Recipe: Malawach* — 108

## Chapter Four

### Rejoice: *How We Find Joy*

**Between Guavas and Apples** by Ruth Behar — 115
*Recipe: Mami's Apple and Guava Cake* — 118

**Magic Ingredients** by Deidre Havrelock — 121
*Recipe: Bison Stew* — 124

***I'm Learning How to Cook, so Stop Complaining, Mom!*
Presents How to Make Puff-Puff** by Sarah Raughley — 127
*Recipe: Puff-Puff* — 130

**Sharing Meals Is Sharing a Piece of Who We Are** by Susan Yoon — 133
*Recipe: Dosirak for One or Two or Three* — 137

**A Cup of Shaah** by Rahma Rodaah — 139
*Recipe: Somali Shaah with Milk* — 143

**Glossary** — 144

**Acknowledgments** — 147

**Index** — 148

As a 13-year-old who loves to read and learn about different cultures, I am excited to introduce *The Antiracist Kitchen: 21 Stories (and Recipes)* to you. This is not your typical cookbook. Not only will you find delicious recipes from different cultures but this middle-grade antiracist anthology will also inspire you to have important conversations about racial justice with your friends and family.

Food and culture are intertwined. Each culture has its own unique cuisine that has been shaped by a combination of factors, including geography, climate and the availability of local ingredients. These dishes are not just nourishment for the body but also play a central role in many traditions and customs.

Exploring the food of a culture different from our own can be a powerful way to break down barriers and prejudices. When we sit down to a meal prepared by someone else, we are given the opportunity to learn about their way of life and taste new flavors and ingredients. This can help expand our understanding of the world and foster a sense of connection with others.

The unique smell of the spices at Chefette, a local restaurant in Barbados, and the aroma of fish cakes and flying fish takes me back to my annual summer trips to the island. Those smells unlock memories of sharing yummy meals with my family, specifically my grandparents. There might be baked picnic ham and fish cakes for breakfast, roasted breadfruit for lunch and macaroni pie for dinner. Every meal I enjoyed in Barbados that came from the hands of my grandparents made my heart warm and put a huge smile on my face.

Everyone has traditions that involve food, and almost all involve coming together. When we share a meal, we are able to have conversations and exchange ideas in a way that is often more intimate and personal than at other times. This environment can help break down stereotypes and challenge our preconceived notions about different cultures.

I believe that *The Antiracist Kitchen* is a great addition to any young person's bookshelf. I hope that as you add a new recipe to your list of favorites or a new spice to your cabinet, you also add empathy for people and understanding.

**Ainara Alleyne,**
*Ainara's Bookshelf*

# INTRODUCTION

What if talking about *racism* was as easy as baking a cake, frying plantains or cooking rice? Just picture it. You add a cup each of understanding and active listening, a tablespoon of *tolerance*, sprinkle in community, while freely adding in *allyship*, *empathy*, apologies and *restoration*. Everyone gets a turn to stir the pot. Let it simmer and when it's ready, you have antiracism. And everyone gets a helping. Sounds easy, right?

When I was a child, this is what racism looked like for me:

Some children excluded me or did not want to be my friend.

I was called mean names.

People believed negative things about me because they had *stereotypes*.

I was teased about my full lips, skin tone and hair texture.

Garbage was thrown at my family's house when we had just moved into a new, predominantly white neighborhood.

I was ignored, overlooked or treated unfairly by some of my teachers. All because I was Black.

I knew that racism was wrong. It hurt and made me feel alone, powerless and invisible. But racism wasn't talked about at my school. I didn't learn about how to stop it or what to do if it happened to me.

## DEALING WITH IT

Some things helped me when I experienced this racism. My parents *emigrated* from Saint Ann, Jamaica, in the 1970s to Toronto, where I was born and grew up. When I would tell them what happened to me at school, usually my dad would talk to the teacher or principal.

My parents told me about the racism they had experienced. They also taught me about Black heroes like Martin Luther King Jr., who was a leader in the US civil rights movement. I borrowed books from the library to learn about Black history since it wasn't taught in my school.

When I was in the fifth grade, I got a chance to write a speech about a topic I cared about. I chose racism. Although I was nervous, it was the first chance I'd had to talk about this issue in front of my whole school.

This helped me, but racism in the world continued.

## THE STORIES IN OUR FOOD

Whether they are forcibly displaced or *exiled*, *immigrate*, *seek refuge* or *migrate*, people who move bring their cultures with them—language, music, customs, beliefs and food. Sometimes policies and systems make it difficult for them to hold on to their cultures. From the 1600s to the 1800s, my *ancestors* in West Africa were taken from there to Xaymaca, the *Indigenous* name for Jamaica, and *enslaved* by English people. In the 1900s most of my relatives immigrated to the United Kingdom and the United States, first as *migrant workers*, then as immigrants.

The food I grew up with came from different cultures. I love to eat. Whether it was the Jamaican foods my parents made or other foods

they introduced to me and my siblings, I loved them all. Eventually this led to a love of cooking. I started out by helping my parents prepare, season, thaw, chop and stir. Because I have a few allergies and I became a *vegetarian* as an adult, learning to cook foods I could eat became essential. Cooking helps me nourish my body and express love.

## COURAGEOUS CONVERSATIONS

As I got older, I discovered that talking about racism can make some people feel uncomfortable, deny that it's happening or even try to avoid or stop you from discussing it. But ignoring a problem doesn't make it disappear.

I want to make it easier to have conversations about the "tough stuff" that comes up when we discuss racism, such as *cultural genocide*, *slavery*, *assimilation*, violence and *discrimination*, which can affect people in different ways for many *generations*.

An important thing we can do is listen to people who are different from us or from other parts of the world. When we pay attention to each other's stories, we can start to care, an important step in ending racism.

I feel like the more we talk about these issues, the more we can heal ourselves and our communities, and find solutions.

Maybe sharing a meal can make it just a little easier to do this. Sometimes the act of cooking can "break the ice." It's a lot easier to listen and share when our taste buds are awake and our tummies are full.

As a classroom teacher, I enjoy cooking with my students. Through making sugar cookies, Haitian soup joumou and hot chocolate, Jamaican corn soup, fondue, crêpes and fried plantains, I have been able to build community and teach about slavery, **_emancipation_** and **_decolonization_**.

These are the reasons I wanted to create *The Antiracist Kitchen: 21 Stories (and Recipes)*. I asked many diverse authors to share their recipes and stories. In these pages you have the very best from across Turtle Island (an Indigenous name for Canada, the United States and Mexico) and the world. The book is arranged into four chapters—reclaim, resist, restore and rejoice, all different approaches to fight racism.

You will notice that many words are written in boldface italics. You'll find their meanings in the glossary of this book. I've included words that grown-ups often use when talking about racism. This will help you to become part of the conversation. I encourage you to read more about these topics.

Asking an adult for help in preparing these recipes is a great way to keep safe, learn and taste delicious food together. Let's get started. Here is one of my favorite dishes from my own culture.

Enjoy!

# CORNMEAL PORRIDGE

**Makes 2–4 servings**

### Ingredients:
1½ cups (192 g) cornmeal

3 cups (750 ml) water

1 cup (250 ml) dairy or non-dairy milk

½ tsp pure vanilla extract

½ tsp ground cinnamon

½ tsp ground nutmeg

½ tsp ground allspice

½ tsp salt

⅓ cup (80 ml) sweetened condensed milk, plus more to taste

### Directions:
1. Add the cornmeal and water to a pot over medium heat.

2. Stirring constantly, cook until the cornmeal starts to thicken, about 2 minutes.

3. Add the milk and continue to stir until the cornmeal is completely cooked and the mixture is thick and smooth, another 3–5 minutes. Add more milk or water to create the consistency you like.

4. Stir in the vanilla, cinnamon, nutmeg, allspice, salt and sweetened condensed milk until smooth and creamy.

5. Divide the porridge among bowls and serve with additional sweetened condensed milk.

# ONE

## RECLAIM

### HOW WE TAKE BACK WHAT IS OURS

**INTRODUCTION**

Throughout history racism has caused people to hurt, destroy or take over other communities through *colonization*, *white supremacy*, war, violence and *genocide*. Racism can also result in wrongful imprisonment, *mass incarceration* and enslavement, causing generations of people to lose their financial independence, livelihoods, lands, languages, cultures, belief systems, *traditions* and food sources, often forever. Racism can also result in people being taught to be ashamed of their own cultural identities.

Today many *descendants* make tremendous efforts to reclaim cultures, languages, lands and culinary traditions that were lost.

This is often possible thanks to ethnic restaurants and food markets that bring the familiar foods from "back home." In most major North American cities, you will be able to find markets that carry food from China, India, the Caribbean, Africa and countries with Hispanic/Latinx peoples and other nationalities.

Making a meal is a way to reclaim the culinary traditions that are passed down to us by our elders and ancestors. For me, an example of this practice is preparing bammy, one of my favorite foods that comes from Jamaica.

Bammy is a flatbread made from **cassava.** I like to eat it fried—it is simple, crispy and so delicious. Bammy comes from the Taíno, a subgroup of the Arawak, the Indigenous peoples of Jamaica. Some estimates say that there were possibly hundreds of thousands, maybe up to a million, of Arawak living in the Caribbean and South America. After Christopher Columbus and his crew arrived in Jamaica in 1494, most Arawak died of disease or were killed. The few survivors were forced into slavery, alongside my enslaved African ancestors, to harvest sugarcane and other crops in Jamaica. I imagine the allyship between these Taíno and Africans and how they had to work together to survive this *oppressive* system.

The Taíno had important knowledge about surviving in Jamaica. We still cook some of their foods, like the famous jerk chicken and bammy, using their methods. Arawakan culture survives today in Caribbean and South American descendants who are mixed with Taíno ancestry. Words like *hurricane, canoe, hammock, potato* and *barbecue* originate from their language.

And although I live thousands of miles from Jamaica, I can continue these food traditions, like the authors you will find in this chapter.

# Beans on the Stove, Corn Bread on the Table

## by Andrea L. Rogers

"You eat yet, Andy?"

No matter when I showed up at my parents' house, that was one of the first questions my dad asked. My dad grew up poor and, sometimes, hungry. He always had a pot of beans ready to share with anyone who came to our house. Whether I was hungry or not, I sat down to eat with him. If I was lucky there was also corn bread—warm, yellow corn muffins that I covered in butter and honey. If you were hungry at our house, well, that was your own fault.

It was only as an adult that I learned how important beans had been in the lives of Cherokees and other Indigenous people for thousands of years. Beans are nutrient-dense, provide a lot of fiber, may lower blood sugar and cholesterol, and pack loads of vitamins and minerals. And in the garden, rather than depleting the soils in which they grow, the bean plants share the nitrogen they produce.

For me beans are a comfort food, a food that is easily shared. Beans aren't fancy, but they're healthy, they taste good, and they can feed a crowd. This year I'm planting some small black Cherokee Trail of Tears beans in my garden. This bean is so named because Cherokees carried it with them when they were illegally forced to leave their ancestral homelands and walk more than a thousand miles to Indian Territory. Fortunately, like the Cherokee people themselves, the small jet-black bean has been able to survive in this new environment—so far. The Cherokee were forced to leave their gardens full of harvests they would never get to gather. But they arrived in a strange new land carrying the seeds that would feed their children and their children's children.

My goal is to grow enough to share a meal with friends and family. Sitting down at a table and eating with my father was a lesson without words. To feed others is to show that you care for their health and happiness. When we gather and eat together, we feed each other's bodies in more ways than one. When we share our foods and histories and cultures, we share something larger than ourselves. I never shared a pot of Trail of Tears beans with my father. He passed in 2011. However, Cherokee tradition holds that our ancestors are always with us. When we grow the same foods they grew, cook the same meals they cooked, we honor their lives. When we sit down and thank them for what they have given us, they are at the table with us.

Phillip Robbins

**Andrea L. Rogers** is Cherokee. She grew up in Tulsa, OK, but now lives in Fayetteville, AR, where she is enjoying being a student again, spending time outside and wishing she had more time to make art and cookies. Her three wonderful kids are the best things in her life. Her writing for children includes the book *Mary and the Trail of Tears: A Cherokee Removal Survival Story* and the story "The Ballad of Maggie Wilson," which appeared in *Ancestor Approved: Intertribal Stories for Kids*. She has also written a YA book of scary stories called *Man Made Monsters*. She believes everyone has a story to tell.

## BEAN SOUP (TUYA UGAMA)

### Serves 8–10

*This recipe can be adapted to be vegetarian or vegan by replacing the meat with 1–2 tbsp of olive oil. It can also easily be reduced or increased for sharing if you wish. Like many things we love, it requires patience and attention, but the results are worth the effort.*

### Ingredients:

2 cups (450 g) dried pinto beans

8 cups (2 L) water (for soaking beans)

¾ lb (340 g) salt pork or bacon, cut into ½-inch pieces

1 large onion, diced

Olive oil (optional)

8 cups (2 L) water (for cooking beans)

2 bouillon cubes of choice (chicken, vegetable or beef)

1½ tsp salt (optional)

## Directions:

1. Rinse the beans and discard any pebbles.

2. Place the beans in a large pot and cover with about 8 cups of cold water. If you planned ahead, cover with a lid and allow the beans to soak overnight. If not, bring the water and beans to a rapid boil for 2 minutes, remove from heat, cover with a lid and let sit for at least 1 hour.

3. Drain the beans and rinse well. Set aside.

4. Add the salt pork or bacon to a large pot over medium heat. Cook until the fat is rendered down, then add the diced onion.

5. Lower the heat to low and cook the onion until translucent, 7–10 minutes. Do not pour off the grease. You should have about 1–2 tbsp of of grease left in the pot. Add a bit of olive oil if necessary.

6. Carefully add the beans and 8 cups of water to the pot. The beans should be covered by at least 1 inch of water throughout the cooking process, so if 8 cups isn't enough, add more water.

7. Turn the heat up to high and bring the beans to a rapid boil. Periodically, stir to make sure the beans aren't sticking to the bottom of the pan. The beans must boil for at least 10 minutes. Stir and add water, if needed.

8. While boiling, stir in the bouillon cubes.

9. After 10 minutes, turn the heat down to low and cover with a lid. Simmer beans for 1–2 hours or until they are as soft as you like. If this is the first time you have made beans, check every 15 minutes to make sure the heat is not too high, the water has not gotten too low and the beans aren't sticking to the bottom of the pan. Remember—water should cover the beans by at least an inch. If the beans are sticking to the bottom of the pan, it is a sign they're burning. Few things smell worse than burned beans.

10. Once the beans are as soft as you like them, turn off the heat. Taste and add a bit of salt if needed before serving. Let cool before placing in the refrigerator.

## Notes:

· If you are only serving a little at a time, you can reheat the bowls individually in the microwave. Otherwise, reheat the whole pot on the stove over low heat and keep an eye on liquid levels, stirring occasionally.

· Pairs well with corn bread or biscuits.

# Love Me, Love My Banana Fritters
## by Hasani Claxton

One of my favorite things to do with my two daughters is playing video games. When my older daughter, Cassie, was about five years old, I got her a princess adventure game in which you can create your own character. Cassie was really into princesses at the time, but I was frustrated that none of the characters she loved looked like her, with brown skin, brown eyes and kinky black hair. Instead all the princesses had white skin, blue eyes and straight hair. I was so excited that her new video game would let her make a princess that looked like her. I showed her how to use the game's character creator and stepped away for a while so she could do her thing. When I came back, she had made a character with white skin, blue eyes and long blond hair.

"Don't you want your princess to have brown skin like you?" I asked her.

"No, Daddy. I want it to be pretty," Cassie replied.

Of course, I think my daughters are the most beautiful girls in the world, so I was shocked that she thought people who looked like her weren't pretty. I began to come up with ways to teach my daughter to love herself and people like her. I found as many books, comics, movies and television shows as I could with Black characters (which wasn't many). Most important, I tried to connect her with our culture. I grew up in Saint Kitts, a small island in the Caribbean, where most of the people are of African descent. My dad was from there, and my mom is from Jamaica. I began cooking recipes from back home to get her excited about where we're from. When I was little, I always loved my mother's banana fritters. They're like pancakes, but so sweet and full of banana flavor that you don't need any syrup.

I encouraged my children to help me make them. They mashed the bananas while I measured out the flour, sugar and other ingredients. Banana fritters quickly became one of their favorites. By the time Cassie was 13, she was a confident and proud Black teenager. She keeps her hair **natural** and wears her Jamaican flag T-shirt every chance she gets. Now she wants to learn how to make other Caribbean snacks, like festival and johnnycakes, because for her, and for many children of immigrants, food is a gateway to learning to love her culture and herself.

**Hasani Claxton** was an attorney in New York City. When he began to take art classes at night, he realized he really wanted to become an artist. He has always loved science fiction and fantasy but was frustrated by the lack of diversity. This inspired him to start creating stories and art starring people who look like him. When he's not writing, painting, showing his artwork or teaching art at Bowie State University, he is probably reading comics or watching anime.

## BANANA FRITTERS

**Makes 8-10 fritters**

### Ingredients:

2 large, very ripe to overripe bananas

½ cup (100 g) brown sugar

1 egg, lightly whisked

½ cup (125 mL) milk

1 tsp (5 mL) vanilla

1 cup (120 g) flour

½ tsp cinnamon

A pinch of salt (optional)

Vegetable oil for frying

### Directions:

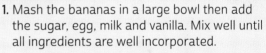

1. Mash the bananas in a large bowl then add the sugar, egg, milk and vanilla. Mix well until all ingredients are well incorporated.

2. In a separate bowl, whisk together the flour, cinnamon and salt.

3. Add the dry ingredients to the banana mixture a little at a time until well mixed. The batter will be a little runny.

4. Heat a skillet or griddle over medium heat.

5. Add about 1 tbsp (15 mL) vegetable oil to the skillet and spread it evenly to cover the surface of the skillet.

6. Pour about ¼ cup of the batter into the skillet and cook until the edges are golden brown, 1-2 minutes, Flip and cook the other side, another minute or two. Repeat with the remaining batter, adding more oil to the pan as needed.

7. Cool on a plate lined with paper towels to soak up any extra oil. Serve warm.

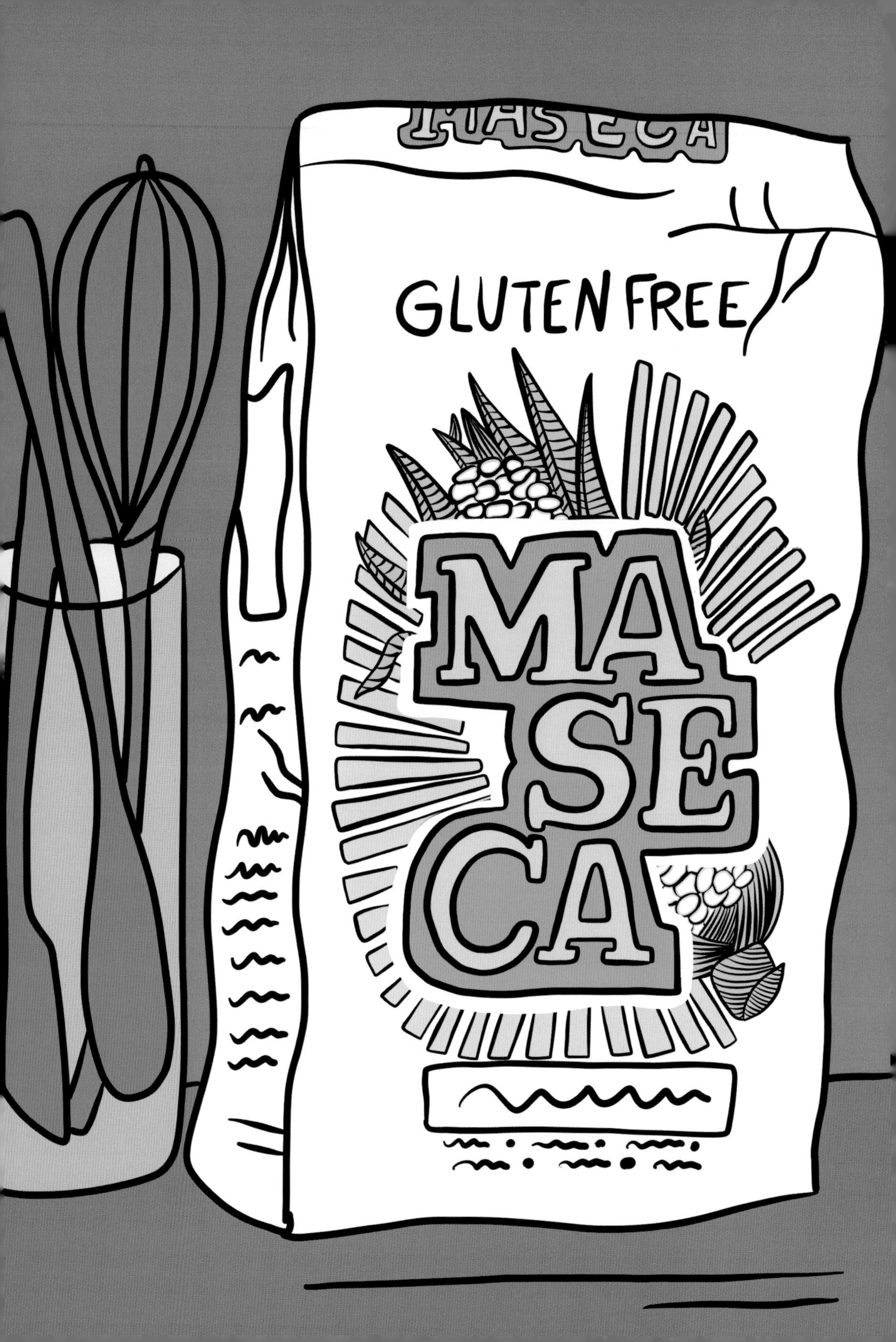

MASECA
GLUTEN FREE
MASECA

# Tortillas con Queso (and Love)

## by Jennifer De Leon

Growing up, amid the loud laughter and chairs scraping to make room for more at the table, the smell of meat sizzling on the stove and my abuela's constant urging "¡Ven a comer!" inviting us to come eat, there was always a bag of MASECA on the kitchen counter.

Whether it was in my house, my grandmother's tiny apartment in Boston or the homes of endless tías and tíos (aunts and uncles) in Massachusetts, California, Texas and New York, the bag of corn flour was a **staple**. In fact, MASECA might be in every Latinx family's kitchen throughout the world. For my family, this was a way of holding on to the tradition of eating tortillas with every meal in our homeland of Guatemala, a country in Central America.

The bag is white with green-outlined yellow letters announcing itself, proud and mighty: *MASECA: Masa instantánea de maíz/instant corn masa flour*. An image of an ear of corn stretches behind the capital letters, and below them, in a smaller font, it reads *tortillas, tamales, pupusas, atoles, empanadas, gorditas, sopes*. Oh, what possibilities! So many ways that masa can dance on the plate!

But here's a secret. When I was in middle and high school, I didn't think too much about this bag of corn flour. It was just always...there. It wasn't until later, in college and graduate school and in my first apartment in the city, which I shared with friends, that a little pang in my chest made me realize I missed it. And I missed it as a young adult in my twenties, while I lived and studied all over the world. So when I started a family of my own, I knew I wanted a bag of MASECA to have a place on my kitchen countertop.

But here's another secret. My husband is the cook in our family, not me. He *loves* to cook. I always joke that even though he is Jewish and from a small town in New Hampshire, his heart and his stomach are Guatemalan. So together, and of course with the help of *their* abuela, we are raising our young boys to love and appreciate MASECA too—specifically, tortillas con queso. Beside us, they stand on chairs at the kitchen counter and proudly stir and mix and assemble the ball of corn flour with grated cheese. "Mama! Look!" they announce proudly. It is part of their **cultural heritage**. Part of our history. Part of our family bond.

Making tortillas con queso has been a wonderful way to continue our Guatemalan traditions. Abuela helps our sons make this recipe all the time, and in doing so, we all celebrate our culture, our community. It helps that the tortillas con queso are absolutely delicious! They are best when eaten right off the stove—hot and blackened and when the cheese stretches as you gently pull the tortilla apart. The smell of tortillas con queso is the part I love best, though. It is the smell of the past mixed with the future and of love moving across generations—and countertops.

Matthew Guillory

Born in the Boston area to Guatemalan parents, **Jennifer De Leon** was often asked, "Where are you from?" This question inspired her to write the YA novel *Don't Ask Me Where I'm From*, about a Latinx teen girl trying to fit in at her new high school. Jenn also loves writing essays and children's books and has won the Juniper Prize for Creative Nonfiction, a Walter Dean Myers grant from We Need Diverse Books, and an International Latino Book Award. When she is not writing, she is presenting at schools across the United States, coaching her son's soccer team or brewing her next cup of coffee.

# TORTILLAS CON QUESO

**Makes 6–8 tortillas**

**Ingredients:**

2 cups (200 g) of MASECA (instant corn masa flour)

1 cup (250 mL) water

½ tsp salt

1½ cups (200 g) grated mozzarella cheese

Butter for frying (optional)

Love

**Directions:**

1. In a medium mixing bowl, combine the MASECA, water and salt.

2. Using your hands, mix into a dough. Add a touch more water if the dough is too dry to hold together.

3. Fold in the mozzarella cheese, distributing evenly throughout the dough.

4. Divide the dough into 6–8 balls, depending on how many tortillas you want to make. Use your palms to flatten the balls evenly into thin disks.

5. Heat a heavy skillet over medium-high heat and add a small amount of butter if using. If you use butter, the tortillas will be lighter in color. If you set the tortillas directly in the skillet without butter, they will become a little blackened in spots, which is my preference.

6. Cook for about 2 minutes. Flip and cook for another 2 minutes or so, until the cheese is melted, and the tortillas are nicely browned.

7. Repeat with the remaining dough, then share!

# Fusion Fried Plantain

## by Janice Lynn Mather

I don't know what I said that day in sixth grade. I just remember Mark's face. He looked like he'd happened upon a strange, new, unpleasant creature, not the girl he'd been in class with since second grade. "Are you *British*?" he asked me in his best snooty, fancy-pants English voice.

We both knew I was Bahamian—like him. I was Black—like him. He was trying to tell me I was also different. It was news to me. I did the logical thing. I hit him with my skipping rope's handles. It did not end well.

We moved on. Mark kept his observations in his head, and I kept my handles for turning skipping ropes, but the words stayed with me. *Are you British?* I knew what Mark meant. *Why aren't you Bahamian? Why aren't you like me?*

I was, and, I began to realize, I wasn't. In our house, Daddy was Bahamian and Mummy was a Jamaican who immigrated to England as a child. My mother quickly lost her Jamaican accent. For years, I clung to her British one. I can't tell you why I sounded like my mother and not like Mark and my other Bahamian friends. Sometimes a daughter is not the same as a mother. Sometimes a girl is not the same as her classmates.

I noticed other ways our family seemed different. One was how we used plantain. In my friends' houses, it was usually allowed to ripen— sometimes until the skin was black—then cut thin and shallow-fried.

Some people let it get really ripe and fried it for a really long time, so it came out crisp and sweet. In our house, my mother peeled hard green plantain, fried it, flattened it and fried again. It is, she always says, neither a Black British nor a Jamaican technique—it's the way *her* mother, Granny Kelly, learned to make it when she spent time in Cuba as a teenager. I liked fried green plantain. Did that make me less Bahamian? I also liked sweet, ripe plantain. Did that mean I didn't fit into my family?

I worked hard to sound Bahamian so I wouldn't be mocked when I had to read in class, so I wouldn't stand out on the stage at poetry readings, so I wouldn't be called a *foreigner* as a young journalist. The Bahamas has only been independent since 1973. Before that it spent hundreds of years as a colony. I didn't want to sound like the people who had literally claimed to own our country. I ate twice-fried green plantain. I ate fried ripe plantain.

Then I moved to Vancouver, where I never saw more than a dozen other Black people in a single day. I didn't even have to open my mouth to be different. Home had never felt farther away. I began to look for the familiar. Finding plantain was like finding gold—rare, and a reason to celebrate. At first I cooked it Granny Kelly's way, green and fried twice. But I missed the Bahamian way too—riper, sweeter and fried black. I started letting my plantain ripen to yellow before I fried it twice. I let it linger in the pan a little. I let those flattened, frilly edges get a little ripe, a little sweet. A little black.

Now I cook plantain a way that is a little like Granny's, a little Bahamian and a little mine. I don't always do things the same way as others around me, whether I'm in Vancouver or the Bahamas. I don't always fit in. I don't always match. I pick things up, though. I learn bits and pieces. I blend and create. I make my own way. Sometimes it's sweet.

◇◇◇◇◇◇◇◇◇◇◇◇◇◇◇◇◇

For this recipe, I put a Bahamian spin on my Jamaican-British granny's Cuban dish. Look for ripe, slightly sweet plantain with yellow skin. You can also try starchy green plantain—it makes an exciting alternative to French fries. Black-skinned plantain is soft and tricky to cut and flatten, but if you get it right, it's crunchy, caramelized magic.

This recipe calls for deep frying, so you may want some help frying the plantains. Make sure that your hands and all cooking utensils are completely dry before heating the oil, as water will make the oil spatter.

## FUSION FRIED PLANTAIN

**Makes 6-8 plantain pieces**

### Ingredients:

1 yellow plantain

Sunflower oil, or other neutral oil, for frying

Salt

Salsa, for serving

### Directions:

1. Peel the plantain and cut it in half horizontally, then into 2-inch (5 cm) chunks about as long as two joints of your baby finger.

2. Set a medium-sized pot over medium heat and pour in about an inch (2½ cm) of oil. The oil is ready when a piece of plantain makes the oil bubble and sizzle. Adjust the heat and take the pot off the heat immediately if the oil begins to smoke, as this means it's too hot.

3. Carefully place the plantain pieces into the oil, standing them upright, using tongs or two forks. Cook 2–3 minutes, then flip and cook another 2–3 minutes, until golden brown. Transfer plantain pieces to a paper towel-lined plate.

4. Stand each piece upright between 2 small plates and press down to flatten and fan it out to about the height of 1 baby finger joint, about ¾ of an inch (1½ cm).

5. Using a slotted spoon, transfer the pieces back into the hot oil. Fry until browned and crisp on both sides, turning once, about 5 minutes in total.

6. Drain on paper towels again and salt lightly.

7. Serve with spicy salsa. Enjoy!

**Janice Lynn Mather** likes to write, cook and eat. Her first novel, *Learning to Breathe,* won the 2020 Joan F. Kaywell Books Save Lives Award and was a 2018 Governor General's Literary Award finalist, a BC Book Prize finalist and a 2019 Young Adult Library Services Association's Best Fiction for Young Adults selection. Her second YA novel, *Facing the Sun,* won the 2021 Amy Mathers Teen Book Award. Her vegan kitchen is crammed with homegrown greens and imported treasures from her Bahamian Jamaican upbringing. Janice Lynn writes and cooks in Tsawwassen, BC.

# Manoomin

## by Waubgeshig Rice

The word for wild rice in Anishinaabemowin is *manoomin*. It's been a food staple for my people since **time immemorial**. The grain has been harvested from beds on waters to feed countless generations in communities around the Great Lakes and beyond. It's a traditional practice steeped in respect for the land and firmly rooted in Anishinaabe **identity**.

I'm connected to this custom in both heritage and name. The people I'm descended from once proudly carried a name related to wild-rice care-taking and harvesting: Manoominii. But, like almost everything else that defines Indigenous identity, that name was altered in violent ways through **colonialism**. My ancestors were forced to translate it from Manoominii to Rice under the rule of Canadian authorities. But now, as a parent myself, I'm reclaiming that name for my children, as others in my family have done.

The saga of the Rice surname in my family begins with **displacement** from the land. On my Anishinaabe side, my roots are specifically Potawatomi and Ojibwe. My ancestors who were the former had to leave their traditional homeland in what became known as Wisconsin because of the US Indian Removal Act in the 19th century. They fled to the north, to what became the Canadian side of the Great Lakes.

It was my great-great-grandfather, John Menominee (one of the various spellings of the name in this alphabet), who was among the first to move to the Georgian Bay area. But to live in another **jurisdiction** that governed the land stolen from his nation, he had to formally register as an "Indian" under

Canada's Indian Act. As a result, the federal government forced him to translate his last name to English, making it thereafter Rice. It's evidence of **colonial oppression** that's carried through to my generation more than a century later.

That motivated me and my wife to reclaim the original family name for our own children. We decided that well before the arrival of our first son in 2016, he and his siblings to come would have Manoominii as a last name. It was a fairly easy and straightforward process when we registered their births. Governments in Canada have made name reclamation more accessible in the recent era of **truth and reconciliation**.

At home we eat wild rice regularly, often as a side or an ingredient in a dish. Every time, we remind our boys of their heritage and why they are named as such. The food and the moniker firmly root them in the land and a culture that long predates the arrival of settlers on Turtle Island. It's a tradition that survived colonialism and now thrives once again.

**Waubgeshig Rice** is an award-winning author and journalist from Wasauksing First Nation in Ontario, a community famous for its maple syrup. He has written three fiction books, and his short stories and essays have been published in numerous anthologies. He lives in Sudbury, ON, with his wife and children, where they eat pancakes, waffles or French toast every weekend with Wasauksing maple syrup.

# WILD RICE WITH CORN AND MUSHROOMS

**Serves 4**

### Ingredients:

1 cup (185 g) raw wild rice

3 cups cold water

1 tsp salt

1 can (12 oz/340 mL) corn

1 can (12 oz/340 mL) mushrooms

Butter (optional)

### Directions:

1. Put rice, water and salt in a saucepan over high heat. Stir and cover with a lid.

2. Bring to a boil, then reduce heat to low and let simmer for 45–50 minutes, until rice is tender.

3. Drain excess liquid and add as much corn and mushrooms as desired, along with optional butter for taste.

# TWO

# RESIST

## HOW WE RESPOND TO INJUSTICE

### INTRODUCTION

In order to survive, many people respond to different forms of **oppression**, colonization and teasing by finding ways to fight back. Fighting isn't always with our fists, weapons or violence. **Resistance**, the act of fighting back or opposing something, also means protecting and continuing traditions, teaching and speaking languages, and keeping ourselves, families and communities strong. Sometimes disguises or practicing in secret are part of resistance too.

Resistance reminds me of an experience I had when I was in the first grade. My teacher, Ms. D., gave the class coloring sheets containing an image of a bowl of fruit.

I pulled out my red crayon and neatly filled in the apple, trying to stay in the lines.

I looked at my classmate's coloring sheet. She had colored her pear brown, and I thought that was so clever. She even got compliments from the teacher. I *knew* that pears could be brown (*and* green), I just didn't know that this color was *allowed*. I thought I had to assimilate. It's true that most bananas—at least the ones packed in our lunch boxes—were yellow and sweet. But *my* bananas? I wanted them to be like the ones I ate at home. I colored my banana green.

"There are no such things as *green* bananas. They are supposed to be yellow," said Ms. D. I stood beside her feeling embarrassed and said nothing, too scared to tell her that she was wrong, that my family bought green bananas every Saturday at the Caribbean food market. That we ate boiled green bananas with yam, coco and dumplings. That my mother sometimes made us drink the water in the pot afterward to build up our iron or to soothe a tummy ache, which she learned from elders when she was a little girl. That green banana tasted delicious in red pea soup. I said none of these things to Ms. D., who may have had **Eurocentric** views and never seen green bananas before in her life. Instead I went back to my desk quietly.

But if I had the chance today, I would proudly color my banana green and tell my teacher all of the ways to eat them. In this chapter, you will read stories about the small and big ways we resist in the face of racism and white supremacy.

# The True Story behind Ketchup Pizza

## by S.K. Ali

Imagine being allergic to...pizza. Yes, pizza. That delicious food with dough, sauce, cheese and toppings (or no toppings if you're the type who appreciates the fine art of simple cheese pizza).

Wait a minute. How could you be allergic to pizza? The entire thing?

Wouldn't you be allergic to the dough? Or the sauce? Or the gooey cheese?

Like, which part of the pizza are you *actually* allergic to?

If you're wondering why I'm asking *you* so many questions when you didn't even say you were allergic to pizza, I'll tell you that I'm using something called a *rhetorical device*. It's when I put all the focus on *you* to think up answers so you don't focus on the fact that *I'm* the one who said I was allergic to pizza.

I'm the one who lied.

I told this lie to the kids in my fourth-grade class. I even lied to my teacher when he asked how many slices I'd be ordering for the class pizza party. *I'm allergic to pizza, Mr. Kerr.* (His eyebrows did a "huh?" dance on top of his glasses when he heard that one.)

I didn't want to admit a "secret"—*Muslims don't eat pork.*

Back in the 1980s, when I was a child, people at our mosque said there were pig products in the mozzarella cheese that pizza restaurants used.

But that was a lot to explain at school.

So I shrugged and said I was allergic to pizza.

Then the day of the pizza party arrived, and I've never recovered from it.

Seeing *everyone* around me eating pizza while I sat there being fake-allergic was torture.

I went home after the party upset. Because here's another secret—I'd never tried pizza in my entire life before, AND IT LOOKED LIKE THE MOST DELICIOUS THING ON EARTH!

(Sorry for screaming that at you. It's another writing device called *emphasizing*. I hope I've emphasized how terrible that day was.)

Sad story short: my mom said *she'd* make us pizza at home. She went to the halal store and got cheese and learned how to make pizza dough and then...put ketchup all over it because it was red, and pizza has red sauce on it. She put delicious spicy ground beef on top before sprinkling it with delicious halal cheese, but let's not get ahead of ourselves when there's something called *ketchup pizza* staring at us.

We kids weren't sure about this pizza. By then we had tried real halal pizza, and this didn't taste like that. But we kept eating it. Because it was pizza?

When my mom learned to put actual pizza sauce on top, my siblings heaved a sigh of relief—now *this* was pizza!—but not me.

Because I had transformed. My lie had given birth to a truth—I had learned to love the wrong pizza.

So now, once in a while, I crave it. Ketchup pizza.

And once in a while, my mom makes it for me. She even taught *me* how to make it just for this book.

Just for *you*.

(That's a device called *ending on a sweet note*.)

Courtesy of S.K. Ali

**S.K. Ali**, the bestselling, award-winning author of several books, is on a mission to write every kind of story she loved reading growing up. After four realistic novels, she's now moved on to writing science fiction and is dreading tackling horror (yikes!) next. She has a degree in creative writing and lives in Toronto with her family, which includes a very vocal cat named Yeti.

# KETCHUP PIZZA

**Serves 2-4**

## Ingredients:

1 lb (450 g) lean ground beef

1 tsp (5 mL) minced fresh ginger

1 tsp (5 mL) minced fresh garlic

½ tsp sweet paprika

½ tsp minced dried or fresh chili pepper

½ tsp black pepper

1 tsp salt (optional)

Flour for rolling out the dough

1 lb (454 g) store-bought pizza dough (or follow your favorite recipe and make your own)

⅓ cup (80 mL) ketchup, or to taste

1½ cups (6 oz) grated mozzarella cheese, or to taste, as determined by your level of cheesiness

½ green pepper, thinly sliced

½ medium onion, thinly sliced

Olive oil for brushing

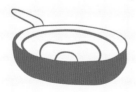

## Directions:

1. Place a frying pan over medium heat and add the ground beef. Cook, stirring, until it has lost its pink color, about 3 minutes. Add ginger, garlic, paprika, chili pepper, black pepper and salt. Continue to cook, stirring occasionally, until the meat is cooked through, and the garlic is translucent, about 10 minutes.

2. Heat oven to 450 °F (230 °C).

3. Sprinkle a bit of flour on a clean surface. Roll out the dough into an oblong/oval piece, approximately the length from your wrist to your elbow. It should be narrow, like 6 inches (15 cm).

4. Spread ketchup evenly on top of the dough, leaving a border of about ¾ inch around the edges.

5. Sprinkle some of the ground beef mixture on top of the ketchup. (Save the rest of the ground beef to make more pizzas.)

6. Sprinkle your desired amount of cheese.

7. Top with green peppers and onion—as much or as little as you like.

8. Brush the edges of the crust with a bit of olive oil. This will make them crispy and yummy.

9. Bake until the crust is golden brown and has risen and the cheese is melted, 12 to 15 minutes.

10. EAT to find the truth of how delicious ketchup pizza actually is.

# Grandma's Greens Chase the Blues Away

## by Bryan Patrick Avery

THE INSULT

comes without warning, hiding behind curiosity.

A blond girl dances across the schoolyard and flops down next to me.

"You're new here. I'm Cassie." She says it as if the two facts are hopelessly intertwined.

I nod.

She clears her throat.

Then it begins.

"Did you know you're our first Black student?"

*I do.*

"Ever?"

*Yes.*

"Do you have a favorite rapper?"

*Um, no.*

"Do you own a gun?"

*What for?*

"Do you live with both your parents?"

*And my grandma.*

"Do you play basketball?"

*I'm hoping to join the robotics team.*

"Does your family celebrate Kwanzaa?"

*No, not really.*

Her questions, a barrage of gunfire, tear through my confidence.

Then, with a sigh, she tosses the grenade:

"You're not very Black, are you?"


## I'M BLACK ENOUGH

I want to say.

But Cassie is already getting up to leave.

I'm Black enough that nervous salespeople follow me through their stores in case I'm a thief.

I'm Black enough that I don't wear hoodies because...well, you know.

I'm Black enough that women clutch their purses when I'm nearby.

I'm Black enough that I still remember the night a sheriff's deputy leaned in our car window and said, to my father, "License and registration...boy."

I'm Black enough that my heart races when I see a police car, even though I know I've done nothing wrong.

I'm Black enough, I try to say.

But Cassie is already walking away.


## DAD WORKS LATE ON TUESDAYS

and Mom works late every day.

It's Grandma who sees past my fake smile, knows something is wrong and, without me saying a word, knows.

"It's school, isn't it?"

I nod, but not too hard so I don't shake loose the tears I've been holding in all day.

Grandma takes my hands in hers and squeezes.

Her eyes say so many things at once:

*I'm sorry.*

*Don't worry.*

*Keep going.*

*I love you.*

The pain of my day starts to wash away.

I close my eyes and wait for Grandma to say something wise to guide me. Something to get me to go back to that school the next day.

She wraps her arms around me and says

—in barely a whisper—

"Let's make some greens."


## GRANDMA'S GREENS

chase the blues away. That's what Grandma says as she leads me into the kitchen.

She piles onion and garlic and ham and greens onto the counter.

"When our family were slaves in Alabama, your

great-

    great-

        great-

            grandmother made greens from whatever she could scrounge together.

Greens are a reminder that we can make a way out of no way."

I chop, Grandma dices, and soon the greens are simmering on the stove.

I think of my

great-

    great-

        great-

            grandmother and smile.

If she could find a way, so can I.

Mom and Dad arrive home together.

The greens are almost done.

Dad asks,

"How was your day?"

"It was a day," I say.

"So tonight we're having greens."

# BRYAN'S OLD-FASHIONED COLLARD GREENS

**Serves 8**

### Ingredients:

1 lb (450 g) roughly chopped collard greens

½ lb (230 g) ham, cubed

½ cup (60 g) diced onion

4 garlic cloves, minced

4 cups (900 mL) chicken broth

### Directions:

1. In a large pot over medium-high heat, combine the collard greens, ham, onion, garlic and broth.

2. Bring to a gentle boil, then immediately lower the heat to a simmer and cook, covered, until the greens have softened, about 2 hours, stirring occasionally.

Raquel Salas

**Bryan Patrick Avery** is an award-winning poet and author of more than a dozen books for children. His recent books include *Black Men in Science*, illustrated by Nikita Leanne, *The Freeman Field Photograph*, illustrated by Jerome White, and the early chapter book series Mr. Grizley's Class, illustrated by Arief Putra. When he's not writing, Bryan enjoys playing the guitar and piano and going on adventures with his family.

# A Cake for My Bully

## by Natasha Deen

The cake sat on the kitchen table, drizzled with pink icing and topped with silver candy spheres. It was beautiful, and it made me nauseous every time I looked at it. The cake wasn't for me. My mom had baked it for my bully. Not *bought* it. *Baked* it.

I was five years old, and for weeks a group of ninth-grade boys had terrorized me and my seven-year-old sister. Commanded by The Ringleader, they waited for us before and after school. They threw stone-packed snowballs, hurled ethnic slurs and screamed for us to "Go back home!"

My sister and I endured, braced ourselves against the onslaught and pretended it wasn't destroying us. I cried every night, wondering what was so wrong with my skin color that it gave people permission to assault me. I went to bed wishing I could be a different color. Wishing I could feel safe in my body again.

When I couldn't stand it anymore, I told my parents. They cried, and I hated myself for hurting them. The next day my mom said, "We're going to find that Ringleader." I didn't want to, but I wouldn't disobey my mom. We knocked on our neighbors' doors until she found out who he was.

I imagined my mom, with a firm voice, phoning and telling The Ringleader to *never* speak those words again and to leave us alone. Instead she invited him over and *baked him a cake.*

I was heartbroken.

She was supposed to protect me. Instead she had told him where we lived.

A few days later he arrived with his grandfather. We stood in a circle, talking. Hesitantly. Then the words and feelings spilled out. From my sister and me, it was fear and confusion. What had we done to deserve this?

From him there were only eight words. "I was wrong. I'm sorry. Please forgive me." He sobbed them through his tears. He begged, kneeling in front of us and clutching our hands. My sister and I cried too.

After the cake had been eaten and they'd left, a question arose. Had he been pretending for the adults—had I been wrong to forgive him?

The next morning he was at school. No stones in his hands, no hate in his heart. Only more words. "Are you okay? Has anyone hurt you? Can I help you?" Before and after school, he was there, our bully turned guardian, protecting us.

Years later I still hear the sound of his heartbeat against my ear as we hugged that day. Every time I think of him, I'm reminded that our stories have power. They can change hearts and turn bullies into friends.

Tabitha Fenrich

Guyanese Canadian author **Natasha Deen** writes for kids, teens and adults. She believes the world is changed one story at a time and enjoys helping people find and tell the stories that live inside them. When she's not writing, she spends an inordinate amount of time trying to convince her pets that she's the boss of the house. Natasha is the author of the Lark Ba Detective series and *Thicker Than Water*, a Junior Library Guild Gold Standard Selection. Her YA novel *In the Key of Nira Ghani* won the 2020 Amy Mathers Teen Book Award.

## A CAKE

**Serves 8**

### Ingredients:

2 cups (454 g) unsalted butter, at room temperature, cubed

2 cups (400 g) granulated sugar

1½ tsp pure vanilla extract

6 large eggs, lightly whisked

¼ cup (60 ml) milk

3⅔ cups (540 g) all-purpose flour

1 tsp baking powder

1 tsp salt

Pink frosting (optional)

### Directions:

1. Heat the oven to 350 °F (175 °C).

2. Oil a 9- x 13-inch baking dish.

3. In a bowl, cream together the butter, sugar and vanilla.

4. Add the eggs and milk and stir to combine.

5. In a second bowl, whisk together the flour, baking powder and salt.

6. Gently fold the dry ingredients into the wet mixture and stir until just combined.

7. Scrape the batter into the prepared baking dish.

8. Bake for 30–40 minutes or until a toothpick inserted in the center comes out clean.

9. Ice with pink frosting (optional).

# The Best Deviled Eggs Ever

## by Andrea J. Loney

**CELEBRATION #1**

In your family, waking up on a holiday means no alarm clock and no school. Just fun, fireworks and your favorite food. But first it means volunteering at the community center picnic.

And sometimes elderly strangers call you by your older sister's name, or your cousin's name, or even some other Black kid's name. You just smile and hand them a paper plate of food that tastes more like it's from a supermarket than a kitchen filled with love (which you know for sure because you snuck a tiny bite of an *un*deviled egg, and now you can't get the taste out of your mouth).

**CELEBRATION #2**

When you arrive at your friend's house, she's waiting by the curb and excited to share her new video game. You're excited too. So she takes you to the back-yard, where her family's throwing a potluck and a barbecue you could smell all the way down the street.

You hope those burgers are ready, but some of the grown-ups are not ready for you. Because they stop talking and just stare. And suddenly you remember that you are the only Black kid on the property.

Your friend takes you to the table for a plate, but there are green olives on the deviled eggs. And, even worse, your friend's mom's best friend runs over to say, "I heard you were coming, so I brought you some fried chicken, and there's also some watermelon and…"

And now everyone's staring at you, and you've never been so *not* hungry in your entire life.

Later, as you laugh and play video games together, your friend brings in a whole bottle of your favorite soda. You don't talk about what happened. But it's still hard to wash the taste of it out of your mouth.

## CELEBRATION #3

As the sun goes down and you turn the corner to your nana's street, you can already hear music thumping, family and friends laughing, and little kids playing. When you hit the backyard, everyone knows you and your name and your nicknames too, and it feels like home.

So you look for Nana on your way to the table. But when you finally get there, your favorite dish is scraped clean, with only two crumbs of relish left.

*You missed it!*

As you swallow your regret, Nana kisses your cheek and says, "Come with me, baby."

Nana takes you to the kitchen, and you're sure she'll ask you to help her bring more food to the table. But instead she reaches way back in the fridge and pulls out a red plastic cup.

"I know you love these, baby, so I saved you some."

You look in the cup, and then you hug her tight.

As fireworks bedazzle the sky, you sit in the backyard with your family and munch on four perfectly salty, sweet and savory deviled eggs.

They fill your mouth with joy. They taste like a celebration.

Deviled eggs are a popular **appetizer** dish in the United States. They're especially popular in many parts of the Black community. They get their name from the spicy mustard used in the yolk mix. My Grandma Inez, who was born in Alabama, passed this recipe down to my mother, and my mom shared it with me and my sister. Deviled eggs always remind us of sharing happy times at birthdays, holidays, baby showers, cookouts, reunions and other family events.

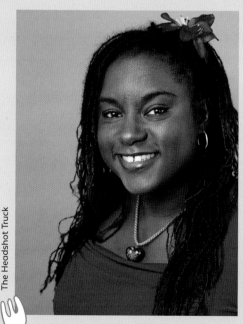

**Andrea J. Loney** grew up in New Jersey and New York, where she spent many happy hours in the busy kitchens of her United States–born grandmother and her Panamanian Jamaican grandmother. She is the author of several fiction and nonfiction books for kids, including *Bunnybear*, NAACP Image Award–nominated biography *Take a Picture of Me, James Van Der Zee!*, the Abby in Orbit series and *Double Bass Blues*, a 2020 Caldecott Honor title. Her poetry is featured in the award-winning anthology *No Voice Too Small: Fourteen Young Americans Making History*. Now Andrea enjoys spending time in her own kitchen in Los Angeles.

# SOUTHERN-STYLE DEVILED EGGS

**Makes 24**

### Ingredients:

1 dozen large eggs

2 tsp white vinegar

Ice water

¼ cup (60 mL) sweet relish

¼ cup (60 mL) mayonnaise

1 tbsp (15 mL) yellow mustard

¼ tsp seasoned salt

¼ tsp black pepper

Dash of vinegar

¼ cup (30 g) diced onion (optional)

¼ tsp garlic powder (optional)

1 drop Tabasco or hot sauce (optional)

¼ tsp smoked paprika

### Directions:

1. Put eggs in a medium-sized pot in a single layer. Cover eggs with cold water. Add the vinegar.

2. Set the pot on medium heat, bring to a boil, and boil for 2 minutes. Remove from heat, cover and let it sit for 12 minutes.

3. Rinse eggs in cold water, then place them in a bowl of ice water for 5 minutes.

4. Gently crack the eggs, but don't peel them.

5. Place eggs back in cold water for 3 minutes.

6. Carefully peel the eggs.

7. Slice the eggs in half lengthwise, scoop the yolks into a bowl, and place the egg whites, cut side up on a large platter. Mash the yolks with a fork.

8. Add the relish, mayonnaise, mustard, salt, pepper, vinegar, onion, garlic powder and hot sauce to the yolks as desired. Mix well. Add more salt and pepper if necessary.

9. Fill the egg whites with the yolk mixture, then sprinkle with paprika.

10. Cover and refrigerate until cold, then serve.

### Notes:

· Instead of boiling the eggs, you can steam them in a steamer basket over high heat for 8–10 minutes and then go to step #3.

· You can experiment with different ingredients. Some people use dill relish instead of sweet relish. Some people use horseradish. You can also experiment with different toppings like bacon bits, chives, capers, cayenne pepper or even an olive. Some people even top their deviled eggs with caviar.

· Vegan? Try Deviled Potatoes instead by using boiled baby potatoes instead of eggs, and vegan mayonnaise in the mix instead of regular mayonnaise.

# Girl Scout Breakfast

## by Linda Sue Park

"We can't do bacon. It's too expensive."

"What about sausage?"

I was in fifth grade, and my Scout troop was planning an upcoming camping trip. Each patrol was in charge of one meal during the weekend, and our group was working on Sunday breakfast.

We had already decided on pancakes, with orange juice, milk or hot chocolate to drink. The budget was tight, and we were debating whether to add meat to the menu.

"Sorry, girls," Mrs. Warner said. "Sausage is expensive too—it costs almost as much as bacon."

I had an idea, and as usual I spoke without thinking.

"Fried bologna," I said.

The reactions were immediate.

"*Ew!*"

"You eat *that*?!"

"That sounds *so gross*!"

I had no idea my suggestion would be met with such a negative response. I felt a familiar dread in my body—hands trembling a little, heart beating faster. From nervousness, I often blurted out things before thinking them through—one of many ways I didn't seem to fit in with my peers.

But this time something about the way my friends were looking at me made me feel determined rather than cowed. Yes, we ate fried bologna at home. And we loved it.

"Let's find out if people will eat it or not," I said.

At our request, Mrs. Warner asked the other patrols, "How many of you would eat fried bologna for breakfast?"

I was pleased to see several hands raised. Although I was the only Korean American in the troop, there were girls from other ethnic backgrounds who were apparently not repulsed by the idea.

Then someone said, "I've never tried it."

"Me neither."

"I haven't either."

Our patrol discussed it further. The clincher was the cost—bologna was less than half the price of either bacon or sausage. We decided to buy a pound of bologna for those who had raised their hands and another pound for "tastes," small bites for anyone who wanted to try it.

The menu was complete.

It *poured* rain for almost the entire weekend of the camping trip. We spent most of the time sodden and chilled, our soggy tents providing neither shelter nor comfort.

Mercifully, the dining hall was warm and dry. Sunday morning, every Scout welcomed the pancakes and the hot chocolate.

But nothing vanished faster than the fried bologna. The room was filled with its rich, salty, meaty aroma. Everyone ate it, the proponents, the uncertain, the naysayers. Everyone wanted more. I felt triumphant, as did our whole patrol.

A European meat product adapted by Americans, transported to Asia by war, then brought back again through immigration...eventually to be savored by a whole troop of suburban Midwestern Girl Scouts.

What a deeply American story.

The people living on the Korean Peninsula endured two terrible wars in the mid-20th century: first, World War II, with occupation by the Japanese before and during it, and then, just a few years later, the Korean War. They were times of rampant suffering, including hunger and starvation.

When soldiers from the United States came to Korea in the 1940s and '50s, they brought their ration packs with them. Many of those foods were eventually adopted and adapted by the local population—foods that included Spam (canned cooked pork), bologna and hot dogs. Koreans were accustomed to making a stew out of whatever ingredients they could grow or scrounge, and during those hungry times, what a blessing it was to be able to add meat to the pot!

Although I didn't know it when I was a child, my Korean immigrant family was following that tradition, which is called budae jjigae—army stew. As with so many foods throughout history, what began out of necessity evolved into preference, and many in my parents' generation grew up loving those processed-meat products. My mom occasionally cooked fried bologna for breakfast even after we could afford bacon or sausage.

Sonya Sones

**Linda Sue Park** is the author of more than 30 books for young readers, including the Newbery Medal title *A Single Shard* and the *New York Times* bestseller *A Long Walk to Water*. She travels often to speak about the importance of books, inclusion and equity. In her free time she enjoys cooking, watching movies and sports, playing puzzle games and spending time with her family and friends. Her favorite vacation activity is snorkeling.

## FRIED BOLOGNA

### Ingredients:
1 package of bologna

### Directions:
1. Place a frying pan over medium heat.

2. Fry each bologna slice, turning over once or twice, until browned, 3–5 minutes total. They will puff up. Press down with a spatula occasionally. They will not brown evenly. That's okay.

3. Eat with pancakes. Or in a sandwich.

# Muhammara

## by Danny Ramadan

The last time I ordered muhammara from my favorite Syrian kitchen in Vancouver, I was disappointed.

The red dip, meant as an appetizer and offered with breakfasts and dinners in Syria, did not have the expected kick to it. Made with roasted red peppers, crushed walnuts, Aleppo pepper, sumac and other ingredients, the dip is meant to be spicy—it burns the tip of your tongue, leaves a lasting flavor in your mouth and opens your sinuses. The restaurant had offered it before, so I was surprised when my order arrived and it was bland.

It looked like muhammara, a single whole walnut on top. It smelled like muhammara, tangy enough to make your mouth water. But it did not taste like the dish I grew up with.

I messaged the restaurant owner and chef—a friend of mine on Facebook—and shared my disappointment. She offered a couple of apologetic emojis.

"White people, man," she said.

It seemed that over the past two years, she'd gotten complaints from dissatisfied customers, saying the dip was just "too spicy." She reduced the spices gradually over the months, yet she kept getting the same complaints. Finally she relented and decided to offer the dip with salt as its only spice.

"But what's a muhammara without the sumac?" I asked. "It's just roasted vegetables at this point."

"Times are hard. We got to adjust with the market."

◇◇◇◇◇◇◇◇◇◇◇◇◇◇◇

I've lived in many places across the world. I moved to Egypt when I was 19, I lived in Turkey for six months, and I was a **refugee** in Lebanon for two years before I came to Canada.

One of the only things that remained the same was the taste of food.

In Syria, Egypt, Turkey and Lebanon, muhammara tasted the same. Always came drizzled with olive oil. Even when I was so far away from home, I still had a taste of it.

In Egypt, muhammara came with Suddoq sandwiches (a type of beef sandwich with spicy dips). In Lebanon, it came with batata harra (spicy potatoes). In Turkey, it accompanied shish kebab. In each one of these countries, the dish that I used to eat back in Syria had been integrated into the cuisine and made a wonderful addition to it.

In each of these countries, no one had tried to change the recipe of the muhammara.

When my chef friend made the muhammara to suit other people, it lost its spices and its yummy taste. It became something else entirely.

That made me sad, because it felt as if something important to me had to change so it fit other people's preferences.

I did not know how to make muhammara myself, so I asked my sister to make it for me. She had just arrived as a newcomer to Canada with her family, and she lived nearby.

She mixed the ingredients, added the spices, tasted the dip, then drizzled olive oil on the dish and offered it to me.

I gathered the reddish food with a piece of pita bread and placed it into my mouth.

It tasted like home.

All I ask you today is that when you make this recipe, please—for the love of sumac—make it spicy.

## MUHAMMARA

### Makes about 3 cups

*Aleppo pepper is distinctly Syrian chili pepper flakes from Aleppo. You may use regular pepper, but if you want the real deal, search online spice stores. If you can't find pomegranate molasses, you can substitute with a mixture of 1½ tbsp honey mixed with ½ tbsp lemon juice.*

### Ingredients:

2 large red bell peppers

¼ lb (110 g) walnuts, roughly chopped, plus a few whole pieces for garnish

¾ cup (90 g) fine breadcrumbs

4 tbsp (60 mL) extra virgin olive oil, divided

1 garlic clove, roughly chopped

2 tbsp (30 mL) pomegranate molasses

1 tsp Aleppo pepper

2 tbsp (30 mL) tomato paste

1 tsp ground sumac

½ tsp salt

Pita bread, for serving

### Directions:

1. Set the oven to broil.

2. Place the red peppers on a sheet pan lined with parchment paper and set under the broiler, turning occasionally, until all sides are blackened, about 20 minutes total.

3. Transfer the peppers to a bowl and cover with plastic wrap.

4. When the peppers are cool enough to handle, peel the skins off, then remove the cores and seeds and slice the peppers into thin strips.

5. In the bowl of a food processor, combine the red peppers, walnuts, breadcrumbs, 3 tbsp of the olive oil, garlic, pomegranate molasses, Aleppo pepper, tomato paste, sumac and salt. Blend into a smooth paste.

6. Transfer to a serving dish. Drizzle the top with the remaining 1 tbsp olive oil, and garnish with a few more walnuts if you like.

7. Serve at room temperature with pita bread.

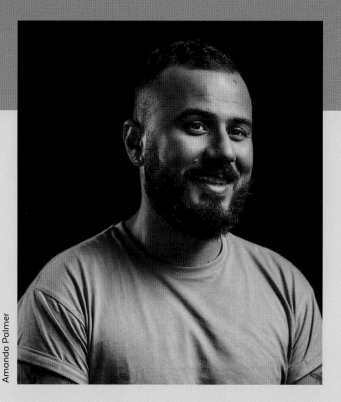

Amanda Palmer

**Danny Ramadan** is a Syrian Canadian author who hopes to leave the world better than he found it. He is the author of the series Adventures of Salma, which includes *Salma the Syrian Chef* (2020) and *Salma Makes a Home* (2023). Danny enjoys playing video games, reading comics and—sometimes—writing novels. Matthew, Danny's husband, thinks that he is clumsy. Freddie, Danny's dog, thinks that he is clingy.

# THREE

# RESTORE

## HOW WE CREATE HEALING SPACE FOR OURSELVES AND OTHERS

### INTRODUCTION

Growing up in Toronto, I've had friends and neighbors from around the world, which has given me the chance to try new foods. When I was a child, I had Filipino neighbors with children about my age. One family had a father who was a chef. To this day, I still remember the delicious new foods I tried and enjoyed at their home—a spicy spaghetti and pork ono ono.

We moved to another Toronto neighborhood where most of my neighbors were Italian families. My friends next door had their nonno and nonna—grand-parents—living with them. They kept many traditions from their old country. "Mangia! Mangia!" their nonna would say, encouraging us to eat. At their home

I tried all kinds of delicious foods—soft cheeses, mortadella (a type of sausage or deli meat) and homemade soup. In the late summer most of the garages on my street were filled with tomatoes for making sauces. Once their grandparents brought home two live rabbits that they butchered and cooked in their traditional way.

My community changed over the years. In 2003 there was an enormous blackout. Most of Ontario and eight American states lost electricity for anywhere from a few hours to four days. My Sikh Punjabi neighbors began to prepare food in their traditional way, using bricks and fire—a way to survive without electricity. They made curried chana (chickpeas), rice and roti (a special flatbread), which they shared with me. It was delicious.

At Christmas and Easter, my Trinidadian neighbors gave my family a gift bag of baked goods—sweet breads, hot cross buns, cookies and fudge. My Sri Lankan Tamil neighbors shared a tea that is good for colds, which I still drink.

For as long as I can remember, my parents have been growing fruits (like peaches and tomatoes), herbs (like mint) and vegetables (like callaloo and squash), which they often share or trade with their neighbors. Many communities have begun **urban farming** to grow their own food, **foraging** to access and prevent the extinction of indigenous plants and opening specialized farmers' markets to increase access to these foods. Being able to grow one's own food, feed others and continue culinary traditions are all examples of **food justice**.

If people live in a **food desert**, they may find that the food options in their communities are unhealthy or unaffordable or both. **Environmental racism** may mean that people lose access to their **arable land** or that the soil in their community becomes too polluted or unsuitable for growing food. Food justice is one way many **racialized communities** restore themselves.

These authors show how we understand each other better when we demonstrate hospitality and invite others to the table.

# What's for Lunch?

## by Marty Chan

I dreaded lunchtime. While other kids ate in the classroom, I hid in the bathroom to open my lunch bag. Other kids had lunch boxes. Cool ones with Scooby-Doo or the Jetsons on the lid. Me? I had a paper bag from my parents' grocery store. The bag was embarrassing enough, but the food inside was humiliating. My lunch was a margarine container filled with chow fun noodles, chewy beef and an assortment of slimy vegetables.

The first time I popped the lid on the tub, the smell of garlic drove every kid away from the table. The few brave enough to stick around and peek inside freaked out when they saw the flat noodles. They thought I was eating worms. I tried to explain that these were like the spaghetti that came out of a can of Chef Boyardee. No one believed me.

That's why, instead of eating lunch with everyone, I ate in the bathroom where no one could see me. Every day, I begged Mom to make me a cheese sandwich so I could fit in with everyone. We had all the fixings in our grocery store. All she had to do was grab a loaf of bread and peel the plastic wrap off a package of Kraft Singles, and then all the kids at school could shut up about my lunch. Except part of me knew that no matter what I had in my lunch bag, I'd still be the target. That's what came with being the only Chinese kid at school. I was the butt of every joke and the main target in dodgeball.

My only friend at school, Jay, invited me to his house for dinner once a week. There I enjoyed a feast. Mac and cheese. Roast beef with mashed potatoes.

Even pizza! Eventually I knew I had to repay Jay's kindness, and I invited him over. I begged Mom to make anything other than noodles. She caved and agreed to make Chinese dumplings. People often call them jiaozi, or potstickers, but I knew them by their Cantonese name: war teep. Sweet pork and green onions lived inside a doughy wrapper. Mom both fried and steamed the dumplings, so they were crunchy and chewy. I loved to dip the dumplings in soy sauce, but I was afraid they'd be too weird for my friend.

When Jay came over for dinner, I sweated the entire time, worried that one dinner might chase him away forever. Finally dinner arrived, and Mom set the plates of war teep in front of us. I watched Jay's face as it lit up after his first bite. "They're like pierogies but with meat," he said. Then he stabbed another one with his chopstick and ate it whole. He finished his entire plate and asked for seconds. Since then war teep has been my favorite dish that my mom has ever made.

Ryan Parker Photography

**Marty Chan** raids his childhood for many of his stories. Growing up as the only Chinese kid in a small Alberta town has given Marty plenty of ideas for his books, which include *The Mystery of the Graffiti Ghoul*, *Kung Fu Master* and *Kylie the Magnificent*. In his spare time Marty likes to create lightsaber effects in his videos, learn magic tricks and play with his cats, Hugo and Minnie.

# MY MOM'S CHINESE DUMPLINGS (WAR TEEP)

**Makes 30–40 dumplings**

**Ingredients:**

1 lb (450 g) ground pork

1 large egg, beaten

½ cup (125 mL) soy sauce

2 tbsp (10 g) finely chopped green onions

1 tbsp (15 mL) sesame oil

1 tbsp (15 mL) rice wine vinegar

1 tsp minced ginger

2 cloves garlic, minced

Flour to dust work surface

1 package 50 round dumpling wrappers

2–3 tbsp (30-45 mL) vegetable oil for frying, divided

Soy sauce, for serving

**Directions:**

1. In a bowl, mix together the pork and the egg.

2. Add soy sauce, onions, sesame oil, vinegar, ginger and garlic, and combine well. Let rest for 10 minutes.

3. Sprinkle a bit of flour on a flat work surface and place a dumpling wrapper on the surface.

4. Place about 2 tsp of the pork mixture in the middle of the wrapper.

5. Using your fingertip, wet the edge of the wrapper with a bit of water, fold the wrapper up and over the meat and pinch the wrapper closed by forming little pleats. Make sure you squeeze any air out of the wrapper as you fold it tightly around the meat.

6. Repeat with the remaining wrappers until all the pork mixture is used. Note: the wrappers can get sticky, so flour the table a few times during the wrapping process if needed.

7. Find a large frying pan that has a lid. Heat 1 tbsp vegetable oil in the pan over medium heat.

8. When the oil is hot, place a few dumplings pleat side up in the pan, making sure they aren't touching or they will stick together. Cook the dumplings until the bottoms have browned, 2–3 minutes.

9. Add enough water to fill the bottom of the pan so that water covers about ⅓ of the bottom of the dumplings. Be sure not to submerge them. Be careful when adding the water as the oil may spit up.

10. Cover the pan and steam the dumplings until the pork is cooked through and the wrappers have softened, 5–7 minutes. The internal temperature of the pork should be 160 °F (70 °C). Repeat the cooking process for the rest of the dumplings.

11. Serve the dumplings with soy sauce for dipping.

# On Belonging

## by Reyna Grande

Have you ever been in a place where you felt you didn't belong? I've felt this way ever since I immigrated to the United States from Mexico when I was nine years old. I felt it in school, where, since I didn't speak English, my teacher put me in a corner of her classroom and ignored me the entire year. I felt invisible and voiceless in that corner. Things got worse through the years. When watching American shows or films, or reading books in English, I felt invisible because there were never any Latino characters. I felt that our stories didn't matter. When I went to college, I was usually one of the few Latino students in my writing classes. *Am I supposed to be here?* I would ask myself.

My insecurity increased when I tried to become a writer. Writing is a career in which Latinos struggle to have a voice, to have our stories published and read. Because the publishing industry is mostly white and lacks diversity, Latino authors are often made to feel we don't belong. Not too long ago I was reminded of this when I went to an author party.

I was invited to participate in a book festival in Washington, DC. The night before, a gala was held at the Library of Congress, the most beautiful library I'd ever seen. The majestic ceilings, ornate walls and marbled staircases made the author party feel magical! I checked in and put my name tag on my blouse. I stopped on the staircase to look at the guests chatting and laughing. I couldn't believe I was there, in the same room as so many distinguished authors. I was grateful to have been included in the festival.

I searched the room for other Latino authors but couldn't see any. The only Latinos I could see were the servers weaving between the guests with trays of wine and finger foods. I became intimidated by the beautiful library and famous authors. I felt that I shouldn't be there, that I didn't belong. Those feelings got worse when, as I began to make my way among the other guests, a white man stopped me and asked, "Excuse me, where are the restrooms?"

"I don't know," I said.

He looked confused, and then he noticed my name tag—just like the one he wore—and apologized. "I'm sorry, I thought you were…"

He didn't finish, but I knew what he was going to say. He thought that because I was Mexican, I must be one of the servers. *I'm an author too*, I wanted to say. *I belong here too*. But part of me wondered if I did.

Suddenly the night wasn't so special after all. Being mistaken for a server at the Library of Congress made me feel like an imposter, not a real author.

But then something magical happened. Dinner was served, and to my surprise, the offering that night was tacos! I stared at the trays of food in front of me and laughed. Of all the things they could have served, they'd chosen Mexican food. My people's food!

As I watched the tacos being enjoyed by all the distinguished guests—all of us under the fancy ceiling of the library—I realized that if tacos belonged at the Library of Congress, so did I.

Ara Arbabzadeh Photography

**Reyna Grande** was two years old when her father went to the United States from Mexico. She was four when her mother left. Then one day, when Reyna was nine, it was her turn to run across the border. She turned to reading and writing stories as a way to heal from the trauma of immigration and growing up undocumented in California. Now she is the bestselling author of several books, including the memoir *The Distance Between Us*, published for both adult and young readers. It was a National Book Critics Circle Award finalist and the recipient of an International Literacy Association Children's and Young Adults' Book Award. Reyna loves to cook Mexican food at home for her son and daughter so that they won't ever forget where they come from.

# TAQUITOS DE PAPA (LITTLE POTATO TACOS)

**Makes 24 taquitos**

## Ingredients:

2 large russet potatoes

Salt to taste

24 corn tortillas

Vegetable oil for frying

Guacamole, salsa or sour cream for serving

## Directions:

1. Peel and cut the potatoes into 6 pieces each.

2. Set a large pot of water over high heat and bring to a boil. Add the potatoes and cook until softened, about 15 minutes.

3. Drain the potatoes well.

4. Add a little salt to taste and mash the potatoes until mostly smooth.

5. Heat the tortillas until they are soft. You can wrap them in a napkin and heat them in the microwave for a minute or two, if you like.

6. Fill a tortilla with the mashed potato and roll it from one end to the other into a tube. Secure it with a toothpick through the middle. Repeat until all the tortillas are filled and rolled. Do not overstuff them.

7. Heat a large frying pan over medium-high heat. Add 2–3 tbsp of oil.

8. Once the oil is hot, place 3 or 4 taquitos in the pan. Fry until they are crisp and a little browned on all sides. Repeat with remaining taquitos.

9. Serve with guacamole or salsa and sour cream. Enjoy!

## Notes:

· As an alternate filling, try ricotta

# Sharing Life's Sweetness
## by Simran Jeet Singh

*Treat others how you want to be treated.*

I've loved this teaching for as long as I can remember. Yet even as a kid, I noticed people only followed it when it was convenient for them. When times get hard, most people focus on themselves.

This is also why I loved learning about Ravi Singh. He leads a **humanitarian** organization called Khalsa Aid and has become known around the world for risking his own life to help people whose lives are in danger. He goes where other humanitarians won't go, including natural-disaster areas and war zones. And he's been doing it for decades now.

While most people run away from tragedies and danger, Ravi Singh runs toward them. He's become one of my greatest inspirations.

Ravi Singh says he learned the joy of serving others through the example of his hero, Guru Nanak, the founder of the Sikh religion. "I'm trying to follow in the footsteps of Guru Nanak," he said. "He started langar to help those who were hungry, and in doing so, he helped people see that we're all equal."

Langar is a traditional Sikh meal that people enjoy while sitting together. Volunteers cook and serve the food, and everyone is welcome to enjoy it. I have always loved walking up and down the rows, giving food to people, one by one. We call this vand chakna, which means we give to others before we take anything for ourselves. I learned this from my parents as a child, and now I'm teaching this to my children too.

Langar is also about equality. Guru Nanak believed that the same light resides in all of us and that we are all equally divine. He created langar to break down the walls that divide us. Everyone who visits a Sikh place of worship can enjoy langar and sit on the floor together as equals. Whenever I'm at langar, anywhere in the world, I look around at all the people sitting together and marvel at the brilliance of the idea—it's been going for more than 500 years, and the tradition is still going strong.

While serving langar, I often think about Mata Khivi, one of Guru Nanak's earliest followers and one of the most prominent women in Sikh history. I think about how much she loved cooking, organizing and serving langar to everyone who came. I also think about how many people say that langar would not exist today without her.

Mata Khivi is a shining example of selfless service (seva). She saw divinity in everyone, no matter where they came from or what they believed—and she served all of them. I try each day to be more like her.

Mata Khivi is also remembered for a dessert she served at langar—kheer. It's a simple dish to make, and eating it always reminds me of Mata Khivi's sweetness. It tastes even better if you share it with others before you eat. As we learn from Mata Khivi, giving to others is what makes life sweet.

## KHEER

*This recipe is made in an Instant Pot.*

**Serves 4**

**Ingredients:**

¼ cup (45 g) raw white rice, such as basmati

½ cup (125 mL) water

3 cups (750 mL) whole milk

½ cup (100 g) granulated sugar

½ tsp ground cardamom

3 tbsp (45 g) chopped pistachios

**Directions:**

1. Wash and drain the rice thoroughly. Set aside.

2. Pour water into the Instant Pot.

3. Set the Instant Pot to sauté.

4. Once water begins to steam, add the rice and milk. Stir gently.

5. Put the lid on, and set the Instant Pot to pressure cook on high for 20 minutes. Let the steam out naturally.

6. Remove the lid, and stir in the sugar and the cardamom, and continue stirring gently for about 5 minutes.

7. Place the kheer in the refrigerator to cool, about 2 hours.

8. Add chopped pistachios before serving.

Kat Chen & Roderick Aichinger

**Simran Jeet Singh** loves reading, running and helping people. He has two young daughters who are way cuter than him. Simran grew up in Texas and now lives in New York City with his family. He teaches and writes for people of all ages. He is the author of two books you might know, the award-winning children's book *Fauja Singh Keeps Going: The True Story of the Oldest Person to Ever Run a Marathon* and the national bestselling book for adults *The Light We Give: How Sikh Wisdom Can Transform Your Life.*

# In Defense of the Humble Rice

## by Ann Yu-Kyung Choi

"Rice is so boring. Yuck! I can't believe you eat it every day," said Andy, scrunching his nose.

"Do you have bread every day?" I asked.

Andy nodded but seemed confused about why I was asking. We were in small groups in class, talking about how food was an important part of different cultures.

"My mom always burns the rice whenever she makes it," said Andonia. "Our smoke alarm went off the last time she made it. But it's okay because we ended up ordering pizza!"

Everyone laughed except me.

How could anyone burn rice? I told my group that my family, like most Korean families I knew, had a rice maker, and that making rice was just as easy as boiling pasta.

"But that doesn't mean it's any less boring," Andy said.

But rice could be a star! I thought about spicy kimchi fried rice, bibimbap (which is rice mixed with colorful vegetables and topped with a sunny-side-up egg) and snacks like delicious rice cakes. Maybe I could bring something for Andy to try? What food could I share to convince Andy and my classmates that rice wasn't boring?

"Has anyone heard of kimbap?" I asked. They shook their heads. "What about sushi?" Everyone nodded.

"I don't like raw fish," said Andonia.

"That's okay. Neither do I," I said.

I told them that kimbap was a popular food. Similar to Japanese sushi, it is a roll made of rice and filling. However, kimbap is uniquely Korean and with a milder taste, and it can be filled with a wide range of vegetables, meats and other proteins like tofu and egg.

"You could put anything you like inside it," I said.

"Like sausages? Ham? Beef jerky?" asked Andy.

Everyone laughed, including me.

"What about cheese? Wait, what about carrots? Or cucumbers? Yum! I love cucumbers," said Andonia.

"Me too!" I said.

"Do you think you can bring some to school one day?" asked Andy.

I got excited, but at the same time, my heart pounded. What if everyone else, including my teacher, didn't like a food that was so important to my culture and family? Their jokes about rice had already made me feel bad.

"I can't wait to try kimbap!" said Andy.

Pleased to see how eager he was, I wanted to give my classmates a chance to share something that was important to me.

I took a deep breath and walked over to my teacher.

"Do you know what kimbap is, Mr. Young?" I asked.

"I love kimbap!" he said. Then, to my delight, he pulled out a lunch container to reveal two perfect rows of rice wrapped in dried seaweed, with egg, carrot and cucumber filling. I laughed seeing the cucumbers, knowing that Andonia would be happy.

"Not everyone knows what kimbap is. I could bring some for them to try," I said.

"That would be great!" said Mr. Young.

An idea popped into my head. "Maybe I could show them how to make it too."

"Even better!" He gave me two thumbs up.

Back at my desk, I happily started writing out a recipe.

There are two words to describe rice in Korean: *ssal*, which means "uncooked rice," and *bap*, which means "cooked rice." Depending on what you use as filling, kimbap can be vegetarian, **vegan**, gluten-free or meat-friendly. Kimbap can be eaten as a meal or as a snack and the best part: you can eat it with your hands. No fork or chopsticks needed!

John Burridge

**Ann Yu-Kyung Choi** is a Toronto-based author and educator. She immigrated to Canada from South Korea as a child. Her third-grade teacher suggested that Ann write to her to practice her writing skills. Forty-five years later they continue to be pen pals. Ann dedicated her children's picture book, *Once Upon An Hour*, to that teacher in appreciation of their continued friendship. As an educator, one of the biggest things that excites her is discovering diverse and unique books to share with her students.

## TASTY AND EASY KIMBAP

**Makes 6 rolls**

### Ingredients:
6 sheets dried seaweed sheets (often called gim* or nori)

4 cups (750 g) cooked short-grain rice

### Some Filling Ideas:
1 large carrot, thinly chopped

Spinach (raw or blanched)

1 cucumber, cut into long, thin strips

Pickled yellow radish, cut into long strips

Kimchi

2 eggs cooked like an omelet and cut into long strips

Crab meat

BBQ steak, cut into strips

Bulgogi (Korean-style marinated grilled beef)

Cooked ground beef

Canned tuna

Fried tofu

### Directions:
1. Place a sheet of gim on a bamboo mat set up so the lines of the mat are horizontal. If you don't have a bamboo mat, you can place the gim on a flat, clean surface.

2. Spread a thin layer of rice to cover the gim, leaving a 1-inch (2.5 cm) rice-free border around the edges.

3. Place your fillings in a straight line horizontally across the middle of the rice.

4. Using both hands, start at the edge closest to you, and roll the gim (and bamboo mat if using) up and over the fillings to make a long roll. Make sure you squeeze tightly as you go and that the gim overlaps a little, so all of the ingredients stay inside. This may take some practice!

5. Cut the roll into bite-sized slices.

*Gim is vegan as it falls under the category of sea vegetables.*

# A Reimagined Malawach

## by Ayelet Tsabari

Everybody I knew loved malawach. Even the non-Yemeni kids who turned up their noses at the pungent tang of fenugreek and garlic in Yemeni soup, who said disapprovingly that jichnoon—a traditional Yemeni Shabbat bread that I loved—was too oily, too fattening and "so unhealthy!" Or that they just couldn't *handle* spicy food, and wasn't all Yemeni food spicy?

I began to announce, "I don't like spicy food," as if my intolerance was some kind of honor, as if it made me more like them. At dinners at my grand-mother's house, I refused the Yemeni soup and started to dislike the smell of it myself.

But malawach was a different story. "Does your mother make it every Shabbat?" my friends inquired with shiny eyes. Bolder ones asked to be invited to our Shabbat breakfast. A fried flatbread made of layers of puff pastry, malawach is meant to be eaten by hand, torn between fingers and emitting a delicious-smelling swirl of steam in the process. Traditionally it is served with boiled eggs, grated tomato and schug (a condiment made of cilantro, garlic and chilies). But most kids prefer it with honey—simple, mildly sweet and oh so delicious!

In Yemen, it is a staple Jewish dish. Since Jews don't cook on Shabbat, they prepare jichnoon on Friday, layer it in a pot and bake it overnight. The leftover dough is flattened and fried as malawach. In my house we ate it alongside jichnoon at Shabbat breakfast.

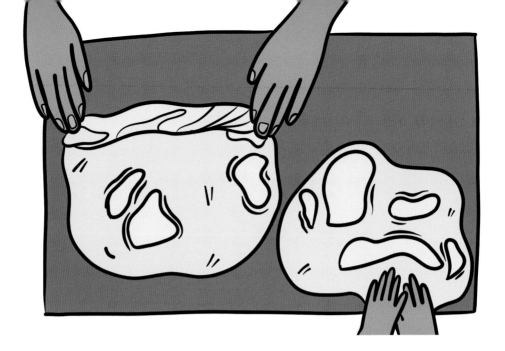

Only after I grew up and tried to make malawach myself did I realize how hard my mother had worked to make it for us every Shabbat, her hands always glistening with oil. The dough had to be kneaded and punched, left to rest and then kneaded again over hours, sometimes days. Each malawach was then frozen between sheets of parchment paper and fried in its frozen state to give it its crispy, flaky texture. I also learned that, like many children's favorites, it isn't particularly healthy.

When I discovered a healthier, gluten-free variation made with rice paper (and, yes, much easier to make!), I had to try it. My mother would never approve (so let's not tell her, okay?). "Rice paper?" She would frown. "There was no such thing in Yemen!" Growing up in Israel, I never saw rice paper in stores, and I know the same was true in Canada at that time, but nowadays, fortunately, this Vietnamese staple is widely available.

These days when I crave a slice of my childhood, I make this reimagined version of malawach for my family. I dip my malawach in maple syrup (after living in Canada for so long, I prefer it over honey). When I really want to shake things up, I stir a little bit of schug into my maple syrup, so that the dish is both sweet and spicy, both old and new, representing a blend of cultures and traditions, just like me and my mixed family.

Two of **Ayelet Tsabari's** favorite things are stories and food. She believes food can bring us together, that sharing food is a way of showing love, and her favorite room in the house is the kitchen. She's also passionate about books and writing, and sometimes she writes stories that make people hungry. She is the author of *The Best Place on Earth* and *The Art of Leaving* and now lives in Tel Aviv with her Israeli Canadian family.

**Makes 5–6**

*You will need an adult to help you with some of the steps in the recipe. The rice papers I use contain white rice flour, tapioca flour, salt and water. They are the same ones you'd use to make Vietnamese salad rolls.*

## Ingredients:

2 eggs

½ cup (125 mL) milk

¼ cup (60 mL) water

1–2 tbsp (15–30 ml) maple syrup or honey

Pinch of salt

18 round rice papers

Olive oil and butter for frying

Maple syrup, for serving

## Directions:

1. Choose a bowl or a dish wide enough that it can fit the sheets of rice paper when they are flat. I use a round pie pan for that.

2. Whisk together the eggs, milk, water, maple syrup or honey, and salt in the dish.

3. Immerse one sheet of rice paper into the mixture. After a few seconds, add a second sheet right on top of the first, then add a third. Let them soak for a short time, just until they get soft. Don't keep them soaking for too long or they will get chewy. Too little and they will be too hard. I find around 30 seconds works well.

4. Heat a nonstick pan over medium-high heat. Add about 1½ tsp olive oil and 1 tsp butter. The butter will help make the malawach crispier, but if you prefer oil alone, that will work well too.

5. Pull the three sheets (which would now be stuck together into one) out of the mixture and place in the hot pan. It's okay if the sheets are a bit wrinkly and not perfectly flat. In fact, these wrinkles make for browned, crispy bits.

6. Fry for 2 minutes on one side then turn and fry for 1–2 minutes on the other side. The malawach may swell and rise. That's okay.

7. Repeat with the remaining rice papers and egg mixture, adding oil and/or butter to the pan as needed.

8. Serve warm with maple syrup if desired!

## Substitutions:

· Malawach is traditionally served with a boiled egg, grated tomato, spicy schug or honey/maple syrup. But it can also be served with other Middle Eastern dips such as labneh, tahini, baba ghanoush, matbucha and muhammara, and even with non-Middle Eastern dishes like salsa or pico de gallo.

· Some people prefer to make it into a wrap. To do that spread grated tomato in the middle, sliced egg, or any spread of your choice, roll and eat.

· You can use water or any non-dairy milk instead of milk.

· You can omit the honey/maple syrup if you don't want it to be sweet (it's not overly sweet as it is!).

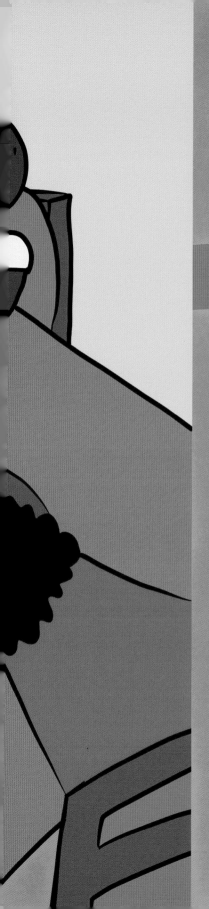

# FOUR

## REJOICE

### HOW WE FIND JOY

**INTRODUCTION**

Joy, humor and play are some of the ways communities have fought against and survived racism. For people who emigrate or flee from their homelands, familiar foods and celebrations often can bring back the flavors and familiarity of home. Sometimes foods and cooking techniques provide clues about how our ancestors lived and what they had to do to survive. Some foods are eaten in times of struggle or poverty yet have made their way onto our plates today in times of celebration.

I am a vegetarian, and at one point I was a vegan, but most of the food I ate growing up was Jamaican food cooked with meat. Jamaican people have roots in many parts of the world, and some of the dishes I love best reflect that history—mangoes, curried chicken and curried goat (India); ackee, yams, duckanoo (also called blue draws and tie leaf) and sorrel (West Africa); and porridge, patties, bun and cheese (England).

A few of my favorite foods growing up were ones my enslaved ancestors would have eaten for survival. Some of us may think these survival foods are gross or disgusting—for example, mannish water, oxtail and cow foot. Mannish water, or what I called goat-belly soup, was a food my parents sometimes made. During slavery, the slave masters and owners took the preferred, more nutritious meats and left the unwanted parts (the **offal**) for my enslaved African ancestors to eat. Sometimes these parts looked and smelled bad. With no other options, my ancestors had to eat them to survive. To nourish their families, they took these items and made them delicious by adding spices and hot peppers and cooking them in different ways. Many generations later, we are still cooking these dishes, and they have become delicacies. Although goat-belly soup, oxtail and cow foot took a long time to make and did not smell very good while they were cooking, they tasted delicious as they were made with love. Growing up, we often ate these special dishes on Saturdays and Sundays.

Today restaurants, fairs and festivals remind us that certain cultural traditions and foods like garlic, tomatoes, strawberries and yams need to be celebrated, shared and enjoyed. In this chapter, you will find ways that foods bring us joy even in the face of racism.

# Between Guavas and Apples

### by Ruth Behar

Growing up in New York in a Cuban immigrant family, I learned that you could make a simple and delicious dessert just by combining a slice of thick guava paste, or pasta de guayaba, with a chunk of cream cheese and eating it on a crispy round cracker called a galleta cubana.

I was too young when I arrived from Cuba to remember what a guava fruit looked or tasted like. It wasn't until I returned to visit Cuba as an adult that I ate the actual fruit and discovered how messy and full of seeds it is, with a smell so sweet it's hard to describe. Once the fruit is mixed with sugar and boiled down to make a gooey rectangular slab, it becomes a unique concoction that can travel for miles and keep for months, the perfect food for immigrants, travelers and those who live on islands like Cuba and don't have refrigerators.

Mami always made sure to pick up some pasta de guayaba, and guava jam too, whenever we went to the Latino bodegas on Roosevelt Avenue. Guava was comfort food for us, a reminder that we came from an island in the Caribbean where the evening breezes felt soft against our skin and a rainy day could turn to a sunset surprising us with a double rainbow.

I loved guava paste and assumed everyone enjoyed it as much as we did. But as an immigrant child, still learning English and trying to fit into American culture, I soon learned that eating a cracker with guava and cream cheese didn't count as a dessert for most people who considered themselves Americans. And not only that, most people didn't know what pasta de guayaba

was, and when I tried to describe it, they scowled because it didn't sound appetizing to them.

The fruit I was supposed to like was the apple. It was the all-American fruit. And the best-known American dessert, of course, was apple pie. But the first time I tried a slice of apple pie, I wasn't too impressed. The crust was mushy, and the apples in the pie were soggy and didn't taste sweet enough.

But as a fruit, apples were good, though they felt exotic to us. We never ate apples in Cuba—as a fruit of cold northern lands, they don't grow in the tropics. Apples, I discovered, were delicious if dipped in honey. That's what we did on the Jewish New Year, or Rosh Hashanah, after we reached New York, to hope for a sweet new year—dipped slices of apples in honey, an adopted tradition I grew up with since my family is both Jewish and Cuban.

So when Mami started making apple and guava cake after we'd been in the United States for several years, I realized she had found a perfect way to bring together these two parts of our identity—the Cuban and the American. Instead of being in conflict, apple and guava can live peacefully and taste delicious joined into one cake. I think of Mami's apple and guava cake as a cake that lets us imagine what hope tastes like.

Gabriel Frye-Behar

**Ruth Behar** was born in Havana and grew up in Queens, New York. She is a cultural anthropologist as well as an author and writes books for young people about immigration and searching for home. *Lucky Broken Girl* was inspired by the year she spent in a body cast, and *Letters from Cuba* by her grandmother's brave journey from Poland to Cuba to save her family on the eve of WWII. In her picture book, *Tía Fortuna's New Home*, she explores the suitcase of memories all immigrants carry. She enjoys traveling, salsa dancing and being an abuelita.

# MAMI'S APPLE AND GUAVA CAKE

**Serves 8**

**Ingredients:**

4 apples, peeled and cut into ¼-inch pieces

6 tbsp (90 mL) guava jam

2 cups (240 g) flour

¾ cup (175 g) sugar

2 tsp baking powder

1 tsp ground cinnamon

½ tsp salt

3 eggs

¾ cup (180 mL) oil

½ cup (125 mL) orange juice

2 tsp vanilla

**Directions:**

1. Preheat oven to 350 °F (175 °C). Grease a 7- x 11-inch rectangular pan or a 9-inch springform pan.

2. Fold the apples and the guava jam together. Set aside.

3. In a bowl, whisk together the flour, sugar, baking powder, cinnamon and salt.

4. In a separate bowl, whisk together the eggs, oil, orange juice and vanilla.

5. Slowly add the flour mixture to the egg mixture, mixing just until you no longer see flour.

6. Pour ⅓ of the batter into the prepared pan and smooth it evenly with a spatula. Place the apple mixture on top of the batter, then spread the remaining batter evenly over top of the apples.

7. Bake for 1 hour. Allow to cool before removing from the pan.

# Magic Ingredients

### by Deidre Havrelock

When I was younger, I used to work as an office assistant. It wasn't a fun job. I mostly filed papers and typed letters. One day, after overhearing co-workers talking about the need to find someone to cook an Indigenous meal for an upcoming event, I excitedly exclaimed, "I can do that for you. How about elk?" This hasty decision changed my life, as I was immediately hired to prepare an Indigenous meal for the 1993 International Year of the World's Indigenous People.

My mother's boyfriend, Alain, was an elk rancher, so finding the meat and getting it butchered and inspected wouldn't be difficult. Cooking the meat... well, that was the tricky part, since I had *never* actually cooked a serious meal in my life. But I figured I could just ask Mom for detailed directions—I mean, how difficult could cooking an elk roast be?

The job was exhausting! It was nonstop, mile-a-minute work. I served literally hundreds of people with the help of my family. But I loved every second of it! I couldn't wait to cater another event. So I began practicing. I read recipes, I made meals, and I experimented with flavors. With Mom at my side, I learned how to cook rice pudding for dessert and stew for dinner. I even learned how to make beef jerky. And I enlisted my grandmother, Nellie, to bake bannock because nobody could possibly make this crusty, flaky, delicious baked bread better than she did.

Then I began searching for bison meat. After all, I knew as a Plains Cree person that I should be eating bison, also called buffalo, as this was our main traditional food source. In my search for bison, I found a great bison rancher and a butcher/processor. Next I rented a kitchen and had business cards printed. And just like that, Spirit Region Catering was born!

I specialized in bison meat. I catered numerous events for my thriving Indigenous community, including a political fundraising lunch, a dinner at the local university and numerous weddings at our First Nations community center. The weddings were my favorite events, because no bride or groom ever wanted to order bison (they always chose beef), so I would happily supply a free bison roast just so the newlyweds could taste their traditional food and fall in love with it!

A few years later I closed my catering business and moved away from my hometown. I missed catering, so I started a small restaurant where hamburgers and chicken fingers were typical fare. *Ugh!* I certainly didn't love that job! Looking back, it's obvious the magic ingredients were missing—culture, my family...and, of course, buffalo.

These days I'm a writer. And the magic is back. I write about—what else—culture, my family and buffalo!

For thousands of years, buffalo was the main food source for many Indigenous Plains Peoples. Sadly, during the 1800s buffalo became a critically endangered species. My Cree grandmother never saw buffalo roaming the prairies, but her grandfather Thomas Makokis certainly did. Buffalo was roasted or dried, pounded into **pemmican**, and it was also boiled in stews. Today, our stews aren't exactly the same as those original stews, but the buffalo is the same. This wonderful, aromatic stew that's made in the oven instead of a pot is from Chef Jenni Lessard of Saskatchewan, Canada.

Brown the meat, add the veggies and have a cup of tea while it cooks and slowly fills your home with a delicious aroma. If you can't find bison, beef may be used. If you are lucky enough to have moose or other wild meat, that is a wonderful substitution as well. You can make this ahead and freeze it, but if doing so, omit the potatoes and add cooked potatoes the day you thaw and reheat the stew. Frozen potatoes have an unpleasant texture.
—Chef Jenni Lessard

## BISON STEW

**Serves 6**

### Ingredients:

1 lb (450 g) bison meat, any cut, cubed

4 tbsp (30 g) all-purpose flour

1 tsp dried sage, ground, or 1 tbsp fresh sage, finely chopped

4 tbsp (60 mL) oil or melted lard

4 medium potatoes, peeled and chopped

2 stalks celery, diced

2 parsnips, peeled and chopped

2 carrots, peeled and chopped

1 medium onion, diced

2¾ cups (540 ml) canned diced tomatoes

1 cup (250 mL) hot water or broth

1 tsp salt

½ tsp black pepper, ground

### Directions:

1. Heat the oven to 350 °F (175 °C).

2. In a large bowl, toss the meat with the flour and sage until each piece is coated.

3. In a large pot, heat the oil over medium-high heat. Add the meat and cook until each piece is browned on all sides.

4. Place the meat and any scrapings from the pot into a large roaster, Dutch oven or deep baking dish. Add the potatoes, celery, parsnips, carrots, onion, tomatoes and hot water or broth. Season with salt and pepper.

5. Cover and bake for 90 minutes. Check the stew after about 1 hour and add more liquid and adjust seasonings if needed.

Mike Harris

**Deidre Havrelock** is a First Nations children's author with a big heart for buffalo. She saw her first buffalo at Elk Island National Park in Alberta. And yes, as a child, she had a stuffed animal that looked like a buffalo. Later she started a catering business specializing in bison meat. She even served bison at her own wedding. These days Deidre doesn't eat buffalo as much as she writes about it. Deidre is the author of numerous picture books, including *Buffalo Wild!*

# I'm Learning How to Cook, so Stop Complaining, Mom! Presents How to Make Puff-Puff

### by Sarah Raughley

Hello, my lovely followers! It's your girl Titi, and welcome back to my channel, *I'm Learning How to Cook, so Stop Complaining, Mom!* Just couldn't stay away, could you? Ready for another recipe?

I've been getting so many requests for a baking video, and as a wise man once said (don't ask me who), ask and you shall receive! So, recently my parents took me to an auntie's 40th birthday party in Toronto, and there was Nigerian food galore. Jollof rice, pounded yam, okra soup, boiled plantains—all my favorites, the works. But it isn't a Nigerian party without desserts, and *this* dessert, puff-puff, is my absolute favorite.

Okay, don't laugh. Every time I mention this yummy pastry to my non-Nigerian friends, they laugh and say the name sounds funny. One friend said it sounds like a cartoon character. Actually they say the same thing about my Nigerian name, Titi. It's the repetition, I guess. Ti-ti. Puff-puff. It makes them laugh. *They* laugh. I don't.

Titi is actually short for my full name, Titilayo, which means "one who is forever joyful." It doesn't feel good to be teased about my name, but when I remember what it means, I know I can just ignore them because, hey, I am and will be forever joyful! And you know what? As much as my friends make fun of puff-puff, when I tell them about chin-chin, puff-puff's smaller, harder, crunchier pastry cousin, they burst out laughing. But you know what? As soon as I stuff the puff in their mouth, the laughter *always* dies away fast and the saliva starts flowing. Funny that, eh?

Some folks also laugh at my name, Titi. It's not a name you're used to. So what? Don't judge by a name, especially when the name was awesome to begin with.

So start by getting your industrial-strength swimming goggles and your gardening gloves. Okay, your goggles don't need to be industrial-strength. Actually you don't need any of that stuff, but, see, we're going to be using a lot of oil, and it splashes. Keeping your distance from the frying pan will work just fine. Having a parent or an older sibling with you is probably a good idea too whenever you're dealing with a hot pan of frying oil.

Trust me, it's a totally easy recipe! I used to get a ton of flak from my mom because I wasn't able to cook. Well, learning how to cook should never be a requirement for a girl. But learning how to cook Nigerian food helped me connect a little more with my culture. Both puff-puff and Titi are fabulous names. Guess you are what you eat.

Melanie Gillis

**Sarah Raughley** is the author of several young adult novels, including The Effigies series and The Bones of Ruin trilogy. She was nominated for the Aurora Award for Best Young Adult Novel and works in the community doing writing workshops for youths and adults. On top of being a YA writer, Sarah has a PhD in English, which makes her a doctor, so it turns out she didn't have to go to medical school after all.

# PUFF-PUFF

**Makes 3 dozen**

## Ingredients:

2½ cups (300 g) all-purpose flour

¼ cup (50 g) granulated sugar

1 tsp active dry yeast

½ tsp salt

2 cups warm water

Vegetable oil for frying

Granulated sugar or icing sugar for sprinkling (optional)

## Directions:

1. Whisk together the flour, sugar, yeast and salt in a large bowl.

2. Slowly mix in the water. The batter should be a little thicker than pancake batter. Add a bit more water if needed.

3. Cover the bowl with plastic wrap and a towel and let it sit in a warm place for 45–60 minutes. The oven or microwave is a good place. (Do not turn on!)

4. In a large pot, heat a few inches of oil over medium-high heat. Once the oil reaches 350 °F (175 °C), it is ready.

5. Using your hand, a tablespoon or a small ice cream scoop, drop a small "puff" of dough into the oil. Use a slotted spoon to keep them from touching. Otherwise, they will stick together.

6. Let cook until golden brown, flipping the balls of dough occasionally so they cook evenly, 5–7 minutes in total. Don't worry if the puffs aren't perfectly round. Perfecting the art of puff-puff is a practiced art!

7. Transfer the puff-puffs to a paper towel-lined plate and sprinkle with granulated sugar or icing sugar.

8. Serve hot.

# Sharing Meals Is Sharing a Piece of Who We Are

## by Susan Yoon

What's it like—the future time when you're reading this? I'm in 2022, and in the past two years I've spent a lot of time alone inside—inside my small apartment and also inside my head, which is much smaller than my apartment but holds a lot more. Like what?

Memories. A lot of them. Here's one.

When I was eight years old, I lived in South Korea. I was walking home with a friend after school, and we got to the part of our walk where we had to make our way up and down a small hill that was covered in tall grass and wildflowers. Some people call them weeds, but I think that's just disrespectful.

When we got to the top, we found a spot to sit down. Our backpacks thrown aside, we opened our lunch bags and took out our dosirak containers, each of us with something left over from lunch.

We shared our leftovers and talked. I don't remember what we talked about or what we ate. But I do remember without a doubt that it was one of the best meals ever.

In Korean there's an expression "kkul mat." *Kkul* means "honey" and *mat* means "taste." It's an expression for something that tastes maximum amazing.

This was that.

Could it have been a gourmet meal? Not likely. Our parents weren't rich. Maybe it was a morsel of castella cake? Impossible. There's no way I would have had any leftovers of cake.

It was sharing a meal with my friend that made it the best. Laughing about I don't know what. Trying foods that your friend eats—and getting to know an important part of who they are.

You know the expression "walk a mile in their shoes"? Forget that. Eat a hundred things that your friend eats. I bet you'll get a better sense of who they are.

During the many stages of lockdown in Toronto, I really missed my friends.

One day my friend Lisa texted, **Let's do a picnic! We can each bring a couple of things. Sit far apart lol meet by the lake?**

The lake is Lake Ontario, which borders the south end of the city, the part where I live. During the pandemic I'd sometimes walk there to check if the outside world still existed.

Lisa and I sat at least six feet apart, our hands sanitized and holding home-brought utensils. Paper plates in our laps, our eyes shiny with anticipation, we couldn't stop smiling.

"Oh my goodness, your dad made this?" I said, stabbing another slice of dry, fatty homemade salami.

"Susan, this is soooo good," Lisa said with a brown-butter chocolate-chip cookie in her hand.

In our enthusiasm we had prepared too much food—but we ate it all. It was 100 percent kkul mat.

Bap is plain cooked rice. Banchan is the side dishes you eat with the rice. This dosirak contains bap and three banchans, but it's less cooking and more assembling, so you can get creative with the combinations! Dosirak refers to any kind of packed meal, but there are dosirak containers you can buy that have divided compartments in them (similar to a bento box). You can find them online or at Korean grocery stores. It's pretty satisfying to look at your food all compartmentalized, but any container will do!

Avi Salem

**Susan Yoon** was born in South Korea and grew
up in Canada. She believes the best meals involve
cake, noodles and great company. She is the author
of *Waiting for Tomorrow*. When she's not writing kids'
books, you can find her at her day job writing speeches,
in the kitchen baking cookies or going for a run along
Lake Ontario. She lives in Toronto.

# DOSIRAK FOR ONE OR TWO OR THREE

**Serves as many as you are willing to share with!**

## Ingredients:

1 large egg

Oil for frying

2 hot dogs, cut into bite-sized pieces

1–2 cups bap (plain cooked rice)

¼ cup kimchi

## Directions:

1. Fry the egg in a bit of oil. Set aside.

2. Fry the hot dogs over medium heat in about 1 tsp, until a bit browned, 5–7 minutes. Set aside.

3. Pack half to two-thirds of your container with bap. If you have a dosirak container, bap goes in the largest compartment.

4. Place the hot dogs in one corner and the kimchi in the other.

5. Place the fried egg on top of the rice.

6. Close the lid! You're all done and ready to feast wherever you take your dosirak.

## Notes:

· Be free!

· Substitute kimchi with any pickled vegetable! Half-sour pickles are my favorite, but dill or bread-and-butter pickles are also great, as well as pickled onions, pickled peppers and even sauerkraut!

· Substitute pan-fried hot dogs with fried tofu!

· Substitute fried egg with a slice of processed cheese! (In Canada, you might know them as Kraft Singles.)

# A Cup of Shaah
## by Rahma Rodaah

"A true warrior, like tea, shows his strength in hot water."
—Chinese proverb

When my family and I immigrated to Canada, we had nothing but the clothes on our backs and a few suitcases to remind us of our previous life in Somalia. Thankfully, we arrived in the summertime, which gave our bodies time to adjust to the new climate. My mother told us that our first few nights in our new apartment were spent on the floor, with only a mattress and two sheets to share between the four of us. I have to admit, those days are a blur to me despite my being seven years old. My memory picks up about a few months later, when I started school.

I was the only Black Somali girl in my class, and this reality was very difficult for me to accept. Coming from a country where everyone looked like me and spoke the language I spoke, I felt like a fish out of water. The fact that I knew no French or English did not help matters much. I dealt with years of bullying and teasing for being different. What I brought for lunch was a major source of mocking because my mother overpacked our lunches with Somali rice, lamb and banana. It took my parents a while to understand that tuna sandwiches were adequate and, most of all, acceptable.

Each day after I got home from school, we would sit down for family supper. We would share our tough days and what we were learning in school with my parents. They would try to make sense of all the odds we'd encountered that day and advise us on how to navigate this new world.

Each night after supper, my parents would sit together and prepare a cup of shaah. For years my mother would complain about the tea in Canada and how she missed the aromas and spices of the tea back home. "The shaah here is so weak and has no flavor," she would often say. When she finally discovered a Middle Eastern market that carried the spices she recognized, such as cardamom, cloves and cinnamon, she felt hopeful about recreating the shaah she'd grown up drinking. As a child, I remember watching my parents share a cup of shaah at the end of each day. The shaah would simmer the whole time we were getting ready for bed, and the aroma would fill the whole house. I'd fall asleep with the delicious smell of all those spices mixed together.

When I met my husband, he did not know how to cook many traditional Somali foods, but he mastered the shaah. I vividly remember the first cup of shaah he made for my parents and me—we were all very impressed. Each sip of his shaah instantly took us back home.

As parents now, my husband and I are the ones who get to drink shaah at the end of a long day, and our children fall asleep with the aromas that dance in the air.

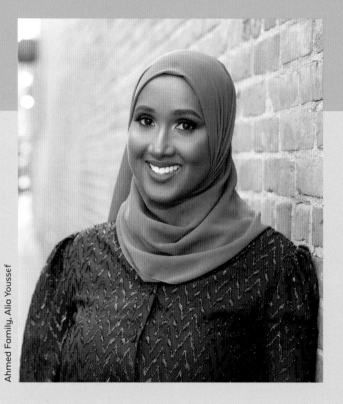

Ahmed Family, Alia Youssef

**Rahma Rodaah** is the award-winning author of *Dear Black Child*. She is passionate about diversity in children's literature and the power of telling your story. Noticing a lack of diversity in the market for Muslim children's books, and recollecting her own struggles of growing up as an immigrant, she decided to write books featuring Black Muslim characters. As a result, she released her first picture book, *Muhiima's Quest*, and her second book, *Little Brother for Sale*.

# SOMALI SHAAH WITH MILK

### Serves 4–6

*If you want a light tea with no milk, add less black tea and cook for about 3 minutes after it boils, but if you want dark rich tea, follow the steps below.*

### Ingredients:

2-inch piece cinnamon stick

10 green cardamom pods

10 whole cloves

1-inch piece ginger, grated

5 cups (1.25 L) cold water

2 tbsp (30 g) loose black tea, or 2 black tea bags

1 organic chai tea bag

⅓ cup (65 g) organic granulated sugar, or less to taste

Coffee creamer or milk and more sugar for serving (optional)

### Directions:

1. Place the cinnamon stick, cardamom and cloves, in a mortar and crush with a pestle until coarsely ground.

2. Transfer the spices to a medium saucepan and add the ginger, water, loose tea, tea bag and sugar. Set the heat to high.

3. Once bubbles begin to form around the edge, immediately lower the heat to low and let the mixture simmer for 5 minutes.

4. Strain through a fine-mesh sieve into a teapot, pitcher or straight into tea mugs.

5. Serve hot, adding coffee creamer or milk and more sugar as desired.

# Glossary

**allyship**—a partnership to fight social and racial injustice by taking such actions as working together to end racism, educating oneself about racism, speaking up or standing up for a marginalized group that is being oppressed. A person who does these things may be called an *ally*.

**ancestors**—the people from whom you are descended, who came before you, your parents, grandparents and others before them

**appetizer**—a small serving of food that is eaten before a meal

**arable land**—land that is suitable for growing crops

**assimilation**—the act or process of being absorbed into the cultural tradition of a specific population or group, often against one's will

**cassava**—a bitter, starchy root vegetable that can be boiled, baked, fried, roasted or ground into flour

**colonial oppression**—the imposition of a powerful group's culture and ideas onto another group, causing destruction of the oppressed group's culture

**colonialism**—domination of a land and its people and resources, in whole or part, in a way that is unequal and usually takes advantage

**colonization**—the process of taking over a land and its inhabitants. It can also refer to the takeover or suppression of cultural practices, languages and ways of thinking.

**cultural genocide**—the destruction of a culture by killing its people and/or banning its celebrations, languages and belief systems

**cultural heritage**—the evidence and items of value of past generations

**decolonization**—the process of dismantling colonization and reversing its harmful effects

**descendant**—someone who is related to a person or group of people who lived in the past

**discrimination**—the unfair treatment of a person based on differences, such as race, religion or gender

**displacement**—the forceful removal of people from their home or residence; a takeover of a position, role, etc.

**emancipation**—the freeing of people from slavery

**emigrated/immigrated**—moved *from* one country to another (emigrated) or *to* one country from another (immigrated)

**empathy**—sensitivity to another person's feelings and experiences

**enslaved**—living in forced servitude (enslavement). People who are enslaved are unable to leave their positions, are unpaid for their labor and do not profit from the work or have control over their own lives.

**environmental racism**—a form of racism and environmental injustice in which policies and practices that result in pollution or toxic conditions disproportionately impact a racialized community

**Eurocentric**—centered on and prioritizing Europe and Europeans; a tendency to reflect the worldview of Europeans

**exiled**—expelled from one's own country or home

**food desert**—an area where people do not have access to affordable and nutritious foods, such as fresh fruits and vegetables

**food justice**—the view that access to nutritious, affordable, culturally appropriate food is a human right

**foraging**—gathering food that is free and grows in the wild

**generation**—a body of people who live in the same period, usually the time between the birth of the parents and the birth of their offspring, and often have similar values and social behaviors

**genocide**—intentional destruction (killing) of an entire racial, ethnic, political or cultural group of people

**humanitarian**—promoting the health and well-being of people, such as providing food, shelter and clothing

**identity**—anything that creates a sense of who you are and makes you *you*

**Indigenous**—of or relating to the first inhabitants of a place

**jurisdiction**—the power, right or ability to make laws; the area or region in which that authority may be exercised

**mass incarceration**—large-scale imprisonment. Known to disproportionately affect racialized groups.

**migrant worker**—a person who moves from one country to another for work, temporarily or periodically, such as a migrant farm worker (also called a *seasonal agricultural worker*)

**migrate**—to move from one place, region or country to another

**natural (hair)**—used in discussions about Black or Afro-textured hair that is left in its natural state, unprocessed and untreated by chemicals

**offal**—the organs (heart, kidney, liver) and waste parts of a butchered animal, usually the less desirable parts

**oppression**—unjust or cruel use of power and control

**oppressive**—unreasonably harsh, tyrannical

**pemmican**—a food eaten by some Indigenous people in North America that is made of dried meat mixed with animal fat and possibly berries

**racialized communities**—groups of non-white/non-Caucasian people, also called people of color (POC) or Black, Indigenous and People of Color (BIPOC)

**racism**—the systemic oppression, hate or discrimination of a racialized person or racial group that puts them at a disadvantage in such areas as economics, healthcare, education, opportunities and politics

**refugee**—a person who flees to a different country to escape war, famine, persecution, etc.

**resistance**—the act of opposing something

**restoration**—the act of rebuilding and renewing something, bringing it back to its previous condition

**seek refuge**—see *refugee*

**slavery**—see *enslaved*

**staple**—a basic food that is eaten or used often, such as rice, flour or wheat

**stereotypes**—oversimplified and often prejudiced ideas about a person or group

**time immemorial**—time long past, extending beyond memory

**tolerance**—fair and peaceful acceptance of another person's or group's differences, e.g., religion or race. They can coexist without a concern.

**traditions**—practices and beliefs passed on from one generation to the next

**Truth and Reconciliation**—a process to uncover and acknowledge wrongdoings, harm and injustices inflicted on Indigenous Peoples through colonization, with the goal of rebuilding and restoring a relationship

**urban farming**—growing, producing and distributing food in cities and surrounding areas; also known as *urban agriculture*

**vegan**—not containing any meat or animal products, including eggs, dairy, fish and often honey; focusing wholly on plants

**vegetarian**—not containing any meat; sometimes may include eggs and dairy products, fish or honey

**white supremacy**—the ideas, systems and structures that uphold the belief that white people are superior to non-white people

# Acknowledgments

*The Antiracist Kitchen* began as an idea—a way to celebrate diverse kidlit authors in Canada. Then in 2020 and 2021, Black, Muslim, Asian, LGBTQ+ and other communities experienced increased incidents of discrimination, overt racism and violence across Canada *and* the United States. Indigenous communities continued to face inequalities and struggles for their rights. There were also changes to immigration laws, which made life difficult and dangerous for many, and I looked for ways of bringing people together across borders, around words. I began to think of this book as a collection of stories, diverse voices and a space to heal. I approached many potential writers to contribute to this book. Some couldn't due to the demands of their own time or simply because the timing of this book and the issues it raises were too difficult. I wish to acknowledge all of the authors who *did* contribute to this book, who wanted to be part of it from the very beginning, who wrote stories that were often difficult to tell and courageously shared from their hearts and their kitchens. I applaud them and feel very blessed that they took part in this book.

I appreciate Ainara Alleyne, her tireless work advocating for diversity in children's literature and the foreword she has written for this book.

I wish to thank editor Kirstie Hudson and the team at Orca Book Publishers for their enthusiasm about this project and for immediately getting on board.

I acknowledge my parents, who worked hard, paving the way for me in Canada, giving me opportunities that they didn't have. Thank you to my siblings, family, friends and writing community, who continue to cheer me on.

I acknowledge God, my creator, for the ideas and inspiration, the strength to persevere through challenges, and the lessons. I thank my ancestors for surviving and pushing on. I stand on your shoulders.

And I thank you, my readers, for supporting my work.

# INDEX

*Page numbers in **bold** refer to recipes.*

*A Cake*, **57**
activism
    allyship, 1, 8, 144
    in community, 55–56, 77–78, 133–134
    talking about racism, 3–4
African ancestors, 2, 8, 112
Afro-textured hair, 17–18
Ali, S.K., 43–45
allyship, 1, 8, 144
American food
    apple pie, 116
    bologna, 67, **69**
    school lunches, 81–82
    southern cooking, 51, **52**, 60, **63**
Anishinaabe identity, 33–35
appearance
    Afro-textured hair, 17–18
    being different, 2, 28, 139
appetizers, 60, **63**, 71, 144
apples, 116, **118**
Arawakan culture, 8
assimilation, 3, 39–40, 144
Avery, Bryan Patrick, 49–51

Bahamian traditions, 27–29
bammy (cassava flatbread), 8
*Banana Fritters*, 18, **19**
bananas, green, 40
bannock, 121
*Bean Soup (Tuya Ugama)*, **14–15**
beans, pinto, 11–12, **14–15**
beef, ground, **46**, **103**
Behar, Ruth, 115–117
bison meat, 121–122
*Bison Stew*, **124**
Black people
    history of, 2
    and slavery, 2, 3, 8, 51, 112, 146
    stereotypes, 17, 49–51, 87–89
bologna, fried, 67, **69**
bread
    bannock, 121
    corn, 11
    flatbread, 8, 105–106, **108**
*Bryan's Old-Fashioned Collard Greens*, **52**
budae jjigae (army stew), 67

cakes, **57**, 116, **118**
Canada
    immigrant experience, 1–2, 28, 55–56,
        72–73, 139–140
    Indian Act, 33–34

Caribbean
    colonization of, 8
    food, 17–18, 40, 115–116
cassava, 8, 144
Chan, Marty, 81–84
Cherokee traditions, 11–12
Chinese dumplings (war teep), 81–82, **85**
Choi, Ann Yu-Kyung, 99–102
Claxton, Hasani, 17–18
collard greens, 51, **52**
colonialism
    colonization, 7, 8, 144
    defined, 144
    legacy, 2, 28, 33–34
colonial oppression, 34, 144
community
    culinary traditions, 77–78
    overcoming racism, 4, 55–56
    sharing of food, 93–94, 133–134
corn bread, 11
corn flour, 21–22, **25**
*Cornmeal Porridge*, **5**
Cuban food, 29, **30**, 115–116, **118**
cultural genocide, 3, 144
cultural heritage
    defined, 144
    food justice, 77–78, 93–94, 145
    halal foods, 43–44
    reclaiming, 4, 7–8, 33–34
    survival foods, 67, 111–112
cultural sensitivity
    dietary restrictions, 43–44
    Eurocentric worldview, 40, 87, 145
    and stereotypes, 49–51

decolonization, 4, 28, 144
Deen, Natasha, 55–56
deep frying, 29, **30**, 128, **130**
De Leon, Jennifer, 21–24
descendants, 7–8, 144
deviled eggs, 60, **63**
dietary restrictions, 43–44
dip, muhammara (red pepper), 71–73, **74**
discrimination, 3, 144
displacement
    of Anishinaabe, 33–34
    of Cherokees, 11–12
    defined, 144
    enslavement, 2
dosirak (packed meal), 133–134, **137**
*Dosirak for One or Two or Three*, **137**
dumplings, Chinese, 81–82, **85**

eggs, deviled, 60, **63**
ethnic food markets, 8, 40, 140
Eurocentric worldview, 40, 87, 145

farmers' markets, 78
flatbread
    bammy, 8
    malawach, 105–106, **108**
food justice, 77–78, 93–94, 145
*Fried Bologna*, 67, **69**
fritters, banana, **19**
fruits, access to, 78
*Fusion Fried Plantain*, **30**

gardening, 78
genocide, 7, 8, 145
gluten-free, 101, 106
Grande, Reyna, 87–90
greens, collard, 51, **52**
Guatemalan food, 21–22, **25**
guava fruit, 115–116, 119

halal foods, 44
Havrelock, Deidre, 121–123
Hohn, Nadia L., 1–4, 39–40, 77–78
hotdogs, 67, **137**

identity
    defined, 145
    multicultural, 27–29
    original family name, 33–34
    and stereotypes, 17, 49–51, 87–89
immigrants
    emigrated/immigrated, 2, 144
    and familiar foods, 27–29, 71–73,
        139–140
    migrant workers, 2, 145
    and racism, 55–56, 87–89
Indigenous Peoples
    Anishinaabe identity, 33–35
    Arawakan culture, 8
    Cherokees, 11–12
    decolonization, 4, 28, 144
    foods, 11–12, **14–15**, 33–34, **37**, 121–122,
        **124**
    of Jamaica, 2, 8
    and slavery, 2, 3, 8, 51, 112, 146

Jamaican
    food, 4, 8, 17–18, **19**, 111–112
    history of, 2, 8
Jewish traditions, 105–106, **108**, 116
jiaozi. *See* Chinese dumplings (war teep)

*Ketchup Pizza*, 43–44, **46**

*Kheer* (rice pudding), **96**
Khivi, Mata, 94
kimbap (seaweed rice rolls), 99–101, **103**
Korean Peninsula
    dosirak (packed meal), 133–134, **137**
    foods, 99–101, **103**, 133
    history of, 67

langar meal, 93–94
language
    learning a, 87, 139
    reclaiming name, 33–34
Latinx culture, 21, 87, 115
Loney, Andrea J., 59–62

*Malawach*, **108**
malawach (fried flatbread), 105–106, **108**
*Mami's Apple and Guava Cake*, **118**
manoomin (wild rice), 33–34, **37**
MASECA (instant corn masa flour),
    21–22, **25**
Mather, Janice Lynn, 27–29
Mexican
    food, **91**
    immigrants to US, 87–89
*Muhammara*, **74**
muhammara (red pepper dip), 71–73, **74**
multicultural
    cooking, 4, 27–29, 99–101
    experiences, 77–78
Muslim, dietary restrictions, 43–44
*My Mom's Chinese Dumplings (War Teep)*,
    **85**

names and identity, 33–34
Nigerian food, 127–128, **130**

Park, Linda Sue, 65–68
pemmican, 122, 146
pizza, 43–44, **46**
plantain
    in culture, 27–29
    deep-fried, 29, **30**
pork or bacon
    in bean soup, **14–15**
    and dietary restrictions, 43–44
    dumplings, 82, **85**
    processed-meat products, 67
porridge, cornmeal, **5**
potato tacos, **91**
poverty and food, 67, 111–112
pudding, rice (kheer), **96**
*Puff-Puff*, **130**
puff-puff (deep-fried dough), 127–128,
    **130**

racialized communities, 78, 146
racism
    and appearance, 2, 17–18, 28, 139
    defined, 146
    and ethnic cooking, 81–82, 115–116
    food justice, 77–78, 93–94, 145
    and reclaiming culture, 4, 7–8, 33–34,
      111–112
    resistance to, 39–40, 55–56, 87–89
    and self-esteem, 1–2, 17–18
    and stereotypes, 49–51, 87–89, 146
    talking about, 3–4
Ramadan, Danny, 71–73
Raughley, Sarah, 127–129
reclaiming culture
    culinary traditions, 4, 7–8, 111–112
    original family name, 33–34
refugees, 72, 146. *See also* immigrants
rejoice
    in community, 55–56, 77–78, 133–134
    in familiar foods, 22, 111–112
resistance
    to assimilation, 4, 39–40
    to racism, 4, 55–56, 87–89
restoration
    defined, 146
    food justice, 77–78, 93–94, 145
    Truth and Reconciliation, 1, 4, 34, 146
rice
    pudding (kheer), **96**
    uses, 99–101, **137**
Rice, Waubgeshig, 33–36
rice, wild (manoomin), 33–34, **37**
rice paper, 106, **108**
Rodaah, Rahma, 139–140, 142
Rogers, Andrea L., 11–13

school bullying, 55–56, 139
school lunches, 81–82, 115–116, 133–134,
    **137**, 139
seaweed rice rolls (kimbap), 99–101, **103**
shaah (tea), 139, **143**
sharing of food, 93–94, 133–134
Sikh religion, 93–94
Singh, Ravi, 93
Singh, Simran Jeet, 93–94, 97
slavery, 2, 3, 8, 51, 112, 146
Somalian food, 139–140, **143**
*Somali Shaah with Milk*, **143**
soup, bean, **14–15**
*Southern-Style Deviled Eggs*, **63**
spicy foods, 59–60, 71–73, 81, 105

stereotypes
    of beauty, 1–2, 17
    defined, 146
    and race, 49–51, 87–89
stews, 67, 122, **124**
Syrian food, 71–73, **74**

tacos, 89, **91**
Taíno ancestry, 8
*Taquitos de Papa (Little Potato Tacos)*, **91**
*Tasty and Easy Kimbap*, **103**
tea, Somali shaah, 139, **143**
tortillas, corn, 21–22, **25**, **91**
*Tortillas con Queso*, **25**
traditions
    defined, 146
    family name, 33–34
    reclaiming of, 4, 7–8, 22
    sharing of food, 93–94, 133–134
    survival foods, 67, 111–112
Truth and Reconciliation, 34, 146
Tsabari, Ayelet, 105–107

United States. *See also* American food
    Indigenous displacement, 11–12, 33
    slavery, 51
urban farming, 78, 146

vegan
    defined, 146
    options, **14–15**, **63**, 101
vegetables, fresh
    access to, 78
    collard greens, 51, **52**
    in kimbap, 99–101, **103**
vegetarian
    defined, 146
    options, 3, **14–15**, 101

wild meat, 121–122, **124**
wild rice (manoomin), 33–34, **37**
*Wild Rice with Corn and Mushrooms*, **37**
worldview
    and diversity, 40, 43–44
    Eurocentric, 40, 87, 145

Yemeni food, 105–106, **108**
Yoon, Susan, 133–136

**Nadia L. Hohn** is a multilingual, world-travelling, award-winning author of several books for young people, including the Malaika series and *A Likkle Miss Lou: How Jamaican Poet Louise Bennett Coverley Found Her Voice*. She is an "artivist" who wants to make sure that all young people can see themselves in books. Nadia teaches kids and adults in Toronto. When she is not writing or cooking, Nadia is most likely reading, enjoying music, watching plays or daydreaming about her next adventure.

**Roza Nozari** is a queer illustrator and writer of color. She is most known for her bold designs and diverse depictions of community and is a firm believer that we should all see ourselves meaningfully reflected in art. In her illustrations, she centers those often at the margins of the art world—BIPOC and 2SLGBTQ+ people, among others. Roza passionately illustrates on topics related to community, mental health and social justice. Through illustration, she envisions a world that is affirming, compassionate and uplifting to all. Roza lives in Tkaronto (Toronto) with her partner, her quirky dog named Bones and her bonus kid, Ollie.

*This book is dedicated to anyone who faces racism and
to those who want to do something to stop it.
I see you. I stand with you.*
—N.L.H.

Published in Canada and the United States in 2023 by Orca Book Publishers.
orcabook.com

**Library and Archives Canada Cataloguing in Publication**
Title: The antiracist kitchen : 21 stories (and recipes) / edited by Nadia L. Hohn ;
illustrated by Roza Nozari ; photos by Rebecca Wellman.
Names: Hohn, Nadia L., editor. | Nozari, Roza, illustrator. | Wellman, Rebecca, photographer.
Description: Includes index.
Identifiers: Canadiana (print) 20220491232 | Canadiana (ebook) 20220491259 |
ISBN 9781459833432 (hardcover) | ISBN 9781459833449 (PDF) | ISBN 9781459833456 (EPUB)
Subjects: LCSH: Anti-racism—Juvenile literature. | LCGFT: Cookbooks.
Classification: LCC HT1563 .A58 2023 | DDC j305.8—dc23

Library of Congress Control Number: 2022950244

**Summary**: This illustrated nonfiction anthology is a collection of stories and recipes
about antiracism from 21 North American children's authors.

Orca Book Publishers is committed to reducing the consumption of nonrenewable resources in the
production of our books. We make every effort to use materials that support a sustainable future.

Orca Book Publishers gratefully acknowledges the support for its publishing programs provided by the
following agencies: the Government of Canada, the Canada Council for the Arts and the Province of
British Columbia through the BC Arts Council and the Book Publishing Tax Credit.

Cover and interior artwork by Roza Nozari
Design by Rachel Page
Edited by Kirstie Hudson
Foreword by Ainara Alleyne

Printed and bound in South Korea.

26  25  24  23 • 1  2  3  4